UNKNOWN TURKEY

★ ★

Anatolia, Cappadocia, The Eastern Frontiers

GEORGES PILLEMENT

UNKNOWN TURKEY

★ ★

Anatolia, Cappadocia, The Eastern Frontiers

Archaeological itineraries
with 32 photographs

Translated from the original French
by
BARBARA WHELPTON

JOHNSON
LONDON

GEORGES PILLEMENT © 1974

First Edition in the English Language
Published 1974
Originally published in French
by Editions Albin Michel, Paris

ISBN 0 85307 129 2

SET IN 11 ON 12 POINT BASKERVILLE, PRINTED AND MADE IN GREAT BRITAIN
BY CLARKE, DOBLE & BRENDON, LTD., PLYMOUTH, FOR
JOHNSON PUBLICATIONS LTD., 11/14 STANHOPE MEWS WEST, LONDON, S.W.7

CONTENTS

ILLUSTRATIONS

6

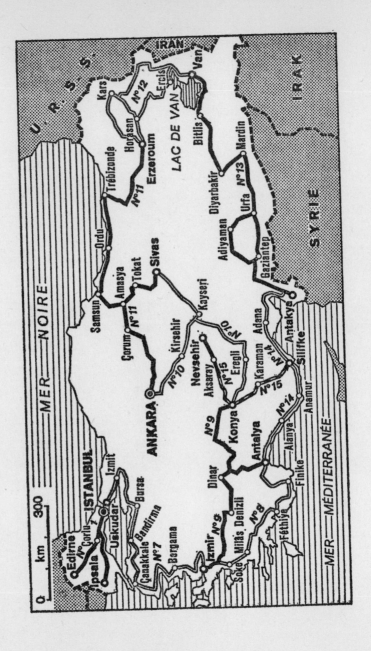

LIST OF ITINERARIES

I

FROM IZMIR TO ANTALYA AND KONYA

SELÇUK (EPHESUS) — AYDIN — TRALLES — SULTAN-
HISAR — NYSA — APHRODISIAS — LAODICEA —
PAMUKKALE (HIERAPOLIS) — DENIZLI — AK HAN —
ISPARTA — EGRIDIR — AKŞEHIR — KONYA —
BURDUR — TERMESSOS

*This itinerary, which enables us, from Izmir, to reach Konya
and Cappadocia, reveals some of the essential beauties of
Turkey to us. To begin with, as far as ancient Hellenistic
cities are concerned, there is APHRODISIAS where magnificent monuments have recently been discovered buried beneath
the soil; the stadium, the baths, the Temple of Aphrodite, the
Odeon and the Theatre, not to mention a number of other
buildings often in a perfect state of preservation and some
admirable sculpture. On no account miss TRALLES which
has not yet been excavated, HIERAPOLIS where the ruins are
set against the extraordinary limestone formations of
PAMUKALLE, the different Islamic buildings at EGRIDIR
and at AKSEHIR and, finally, KONYA where the mosques
and medreses are of truly remarkable architectural beauty.*

II

FROM KONYA TO KAYSERI, ANKARA AND SIVAS

ERIGLI — NIGDE — YESILHISAR — URGÜP — ORTAHISAR
— AVCILAR — NEVSEHIR — AVANOS — GÖREME —
KAYSERI — KIRSEHIR — ANKARA — KÜLTEPE — SUL-
TANHANI — SIVAS

*This is one of the most exciting itineraries of the whole of
Turkey. By following it, we discover some of the most typical*

cities of Anatolia: NIGDE, famous for its mausoleums, its medreses and its mosques, KAYSERI no less rich in Moslem building, usually of the 13th century, which still retains the massive ramparts of its citadel, ANKARA which besides Roman remains has a formidable fortress. But this itinerary also enables us to see some of the strange sites and troglodyte dwellings of Cappadocia with the rock churches of GÖREME covered with very ancient frescoes, astonishing caravanserais, like the one at SULTANHANI, and ancient Hittite cities such as KÜLTEPE.

III

FROM ANKARA TO SIVAS, TREBIZOND AND ERZURUM

Bögazkale — Yazilikaya — Büyükkale — Alaca Höyük — Çorum — Amasya — Tokat — Sivas — Samsun — Ordu — Giresun — Trebizond — Sumela — Erzurum

This itinerary begins with a visit to the most spectacular Hittite sites of the whole of Turkey: BÖGAZKALE, with the ancient fortress of HATTUSA, the bas-reliefs of YASILI-KAYA and, further on, ALACA HÖYÜK and the lovely Gate of the Sphynx. Then follow two towns rich in Islamic build-ings: AMASYA with its mosques and türbes, SIVAS with its two medreses with beautiful carved decorations considered to be amongst the most representative buildings of Seljuk art.

We then continue towards the Black Sea which enchants us by its countryside and has at TREBIZOND an admirable Byzantine church, St. Sophia of the 13th century, which still keeps its astonishing frescoes of that period.

We continue on to ERZURUM by a most picturesque mountain route and find there a medrese which rivals those

we have seen at Sivas and a series of türbes *of outstanding beauty which are also of the Seljuk period.*

IV

FROM ERZURUM TO KARS AND TO VAN

HAHO — KARS — ANI — HOROMOS — KHTZGONK —
DIGOR — TUZLUCA — DOGUBAYAZIT — AGRI — ERCIS
— VAN

Here there is a choice of two routes: the easier one is of limited interest, the more difficult one leads to Armenian buildings which are practicaly unknown, rivals of those to be found at KARS and at ANI. We should not on any account miss this last city, the abandoned former capital of Armenia, which encloses within a circle of impressive walls a dozen really remarkable Armenian churches which are mostly in ruins. The site on the USSR frontier is of astonishing grandeur.

At VAN on the edge of the immense lake we shall see the ruins of an ancient fortress on a rocky plateau.

V

FROM VAN TO ANTAKAYA

AGHTAMAR — AHLAT — BITLIS — SIIRT — DIYARBAKIR
— MARDIN — MIDYAT — HASANKEYF — THE MONA-
STERIES OF TUR ABDIN — MAR GABRIEL — URFA
— SUMATAR — HARRAN —ESKIKAHTA — NEMRUT DAǦI
— BIRECIK — KARKEMISH — GAZIANTEP — ANTAKYA

The first monument which we come to, the church of AGHTAMAR, which stands on the little islet of Van, is the most sensational of all the Armenian buildings of Turkey; the reliefs are astonishing. Besides this, there are just as remarkable Syrian and paleo-christian edifices in the region of Mardin, on the plateau of Tur Abdin, such as the MAR GABRIEL; we shall see Hittite ruins, notably at KARKEMICH, Sabian sanctuaries at SUMATAR and, if we have sufficient courage, we can scale the NEMRUT DAĞI in order to admire the fantastic sanctuary erected by Antiochos I.

Finally, several towns have interesting mosques and medreses: BITLIS, DIYARBAKIR, which still retains its massive walls almost intact, MARDIN, URFA, and we end up at GAZIANTEP which has little to offer save the remains of a fortress, and ANTAKYA which, despite its great past, has only the grotto of St. Peter, the ruins of the fortress and a magnificent museum of Roman mosaics.

VI

FROM ANTAKYA TO ANTALYA

BAĞRAS — ISKENDERUN — TOPRAKKALE — MISIS — ADANA — TARSUS — MERSIN — SOLES — ELOEUSA — NEAPOLIS — KORIGOS — KAYA — ANAMUR — SYEDRA — ALANYA — SIDA — ASPENDOS — PERGA — ANTALYA

This itinerary is one of the most beautiful and most varied that Turkey has to offer. The road which follows the coast, is often cut out of the cliffside and opens up superb panoramas and glimpses of beaches where it is possible to bathe. The climate here is temperate and ANTALYA is considered as a winter resort.

The Hellenistic ruins and Roman ruins are numerous and, if certain towns near Antalya have been excavated to reveal monuments of importance like SIDA, ASPENDOS and PERGA famous for their theatres, there are others less spectacular which deserve to be restored.

We shall also find several remarkable fortresses at BAGRAS, at VILAN KALESI, at KORIGOS, at ANAMUR, at ALANYA, at TOPRAKKALE; Hittite ruins at KARATEPE, vestiges of Armenian cities at ANAZARBUS and at NEAPOLIS.

PREFACE

THE itineraries included in this second volume cover the eastern part of Turkey, Cappadocia, Anatolia, Armenia and the borders of the neighbouring countries of U.S.S.R., Syria and Irak. Ruins recently discovered in Anatolia and elsewhere have revealed prehistoric civilizations which have been totally buried until recently.

During the Chalcolithic Age in the first half of the fourth millennium before our era, the Cilician plain was under the influence of the civilization called the Tell Halan, the name of a site in northern Syria near the Turkish frontier which extended to Mesopotamia and the Mediterranean coast; while in the east of Asia Minor there developed the culture originally recognized at Karaz and Pulaur, where ceramics of geometrical decorations were brought to light. A third culture showed itself in central Anatolia, at Alisar Hoyuk, Alaca Hoyak, and Hacilia.

These had preceded the Hittite civilization, which was practically ignored until 60 years ago. These Hittites were Indo-European conquerors who had emigrated from the Nordic regions in the second millennium. The kings who led them made war on the kings of Kuššara and imposed their hegemony.

We have the chronology of the Hittite kings and the Labarna dynasty, whose capital was Kuššara, then Hattusa and is today known as Boğazkale. It was then the hegemony of the Hurrite nation, an independent branch of Asiatic people, who were neither Indo-European nor Semitic, during the fifth millennium they were then known under the name of Subareens. In the 16th century before our era, they formed a powerful nation

15

which fought against Assyria and the Kassites in Mesopotamia, and also against the Egyptians.

The new Hittite empire founded a little after 1450 B.C. extended as far as Syria and Palestine. In 1278 B.C. the Hittite king signed a treaty of peace with Rameses II, but new invaders towards 1200 B.C., known as the People of the Sea, put an end to the Hittite domination.

It is at the Museum at Ankara where one can study Hittite art. It is there that one can see the greater part of the vases and the art objects in bas-relief which have been taken from the ruins, those of the Phrygians are known by the votive monuments with inscriptions and sculptures hewn out of the rock. The most celebrated is the Tomb of Midas, with its square façade crowned with a triangular pediment and decorated with geometric motifs.

After the Persian domination came the Macedonian conquest in 334 B.C. Alexander, following the battle of the Granica, freed the Greek cities and after the battle of Issos invaded Babylon. After his death, his lieutenants disputed the succession to his empire. Lysimachus and Seleucus took their shares. At Pergamon a new dynasty arose, until the death of Attalus III who left his kingdom to the Roman people.

During this period, which extended from the time of Alexander and the Roman domination, Asia Minor had, under the Seleucids and the Attalids, one of its most brilliant periods in artistic history. The ancient cities constructed their imposing buildings, and the architects of Ionia enjoyed the height of their reputation.

With Christianity, which developed rapidly in Asia Minor, there arose in Anatolia a multitude of churches and monastries, including the rupestral churches of Cappadocia, which we will see on our itineraries.

In Turkey Armenian architecture played a role of importance in the origins of Christianity. In Armenia, the passage way of large immigrations and the crossroads of civilizations, one finds a pleasant compromise between the features of Byzantine and those of the Sassanid empire and its creations, influencing the architecture of all the neighbouring countries. Armenian architecture pleases us with its originality.

It was during the 11th century that a Turkish tribe, that of the Seljuks, ravaged Cappadocia and extended into Syria. The Seljuk mosques, which we can see at Konya and Kaysera, show the prayer hall divided into several naves with ranges of columns and preceded by a court with it ablution fountains. The mosques are accompanied by *medreses* (religious colleges), where the cells and the teaching rooms give on to a central court of hospitals and tombs.

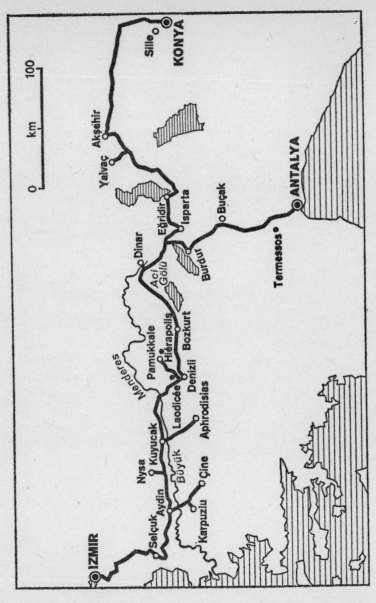

FROM IZMIR TO ANTALYA AND KONYA

ITINERARY I

FROM IZMIR TO ANATALYA AND KONYA

Selçuk (Ephesus) — Aydin — Tralles — Sultanhisar — Nysa — Aphrodisias — Pamukkale (Hierapolis) — Laodicea — Denizli — Ak Han — Isparta — Egridir — Akşehir — Konya — Burdur — Termessos

FROM Izmir we must follow the road to Ephesus (described in the first volume) and, as we leave Selçuk, take the road to Aydin.

On reaching Ortaklar we drive down the valley of Buyuk Menderes, the Meander of classical times. It is the great through route to the high Anatolian plateau across a verdant agricultural region. After having passed through slopes covered with olive trees, the road follows the bed of the great Meander which frequently becomes flooded and where orchards of figs alternate with fields of corn or with stretches of uncultivated land.

This absolutely straight canyon, 200 kilometres long, has a very steep and desolate looking left bank, but a much more attractive right bank separated from the hills by well-irrigated fig orchards. Vines and olives intermingle with fig trees enclosed by walls of earth, here and there edged with hedges of oak or acacia.

At AYDIN, a lively town which is rapidly becoming modernized, there is nothing to see except the *Cihanoglu Camii* of 1756, characteristic of Ottoman art of this period, and the little *Bey Camii* of the 13th century built with materials taken from ancient monuments.

We must now climb up to ancient *Tralles* which was founded by a colony of Argives. It came under Persian domination in the 6th century B.C. until it submitted to Alexander the Great who installed a Macedonian garrison in the city. After his death, it was ceded to the Diadochus of Lysimachus, and then, towards 260 B.C., it was occupied by Seleucus I who renamed it *Seleucia ad Macandrum*. Taken by the Romans after the Battle of Magnesia ad Sipylum, Tralles was incorporated into the kingdom of Pergamum. When this kingdom fell in 129 B.C. it became Roman, together with it. Destroyed by an earthquake in 27 B.C., it was partly reconstructed, thanks to the generosity of Augustus and was renamed Caesarea. A bishopric under the Byzantines, it was taken by the Arabs in 1282, even though it was nothing more than a collection of ruins. It was thenceforward included in Aydin.

In the upper town, two towers of the former Byzantine fortress of Tralles flank the Prison Gate, and on the plateau of Güzel Hisar we can see the ruins of the ancient town. These are to be found in military territory, but it is easy enough to gain permission to visit them.

We can see, rising out of the ground, an entire colonnade which is certainly buried for three-quarters of its height; it used to form part of the *agora*. Further on there remain the two sides of a colossal Roman building which was still standing in its entirety at the end of the last century. The arcading which runs round the building is attractive, but there only remain slight vestiges of the frescoes which used to be easily distinguishable.

At the foot of the Acropolis there is a theatre and a stadium. Since the excavations carried out in 1888 and in 1902 unearthed sculptures now on show in the Museum at Istanbul, we can only hope that new efforts will bring actual monuments to light.

From Aydin we can go and see the ruins of *Alinda* and

Alabanda by taking the road to Yatagan. We first take the road from the centre of Aydin and, after 7 kilometres, skirt the Büyük Menderes. At 34 kilometres we shall find, to the right, a road to the village of Karpuzla which spreads over the site of ancient *Alinda* at the foot of an acropolis still enclosed by most of its walls.

Founded during the Carian migrations, Alinda became, in 343 B.C., the refuge of Queen Ada, sister of Mausolus, who with the ruler of Halicarnassus was the last representative of the Carian dynasty which supported the Persians against the Greeks. During Alexander's conquest, she offered to adopt him as her son in order to hand over the city to him.

From the village, a difficult track leads to the acropolis and the principal monuments of the ancient city which seems to have been mainly constructed by Queen Ada. At the end of the 2nd century B.C., this complex was completed by the King of Caria, Olympichos, who transferred his capital to Alinda.

The ruins are spread out over two hills. The theatre is well preserved as well as the ramparts which rise up on the steep slopes of the acropolis. The solid foundations of the *agora*, composed of granite like all the monuments of the town, stand just above the village with columns which used to support the pavement of the portico.

We regain the route to Yatagan and continue as far as *Cine*, a town to the right from which a little road leads to the village of Arap Hisar near which we can see the ruins of ancient *ALABANDA*.

This town, which had been founded by the Carians, was quite important under Roman rule, during which time it enjoyed the privileges of a free city.

The city, with its walls reinforced by powerful bastions still intact, used to spread across the plain and over two slopes separated by a little stream. The citadel stood on the south eastern slope on the side of which was the theatre with a *cavea*

35 metres in diameter. On the opposite slope there rose up a
Doric temple, probably consecrated to Artemis and which was
unearthed by the Istanbul Museum of Antiquities. At the foot
of the hill lie the ruins of a *bouleuterion*; then, to the south,
those of an *agora*, formerly surrounded by a portico with a
double colonnade.

To the south west, near the market, stood the celebrated
Temple of Apollo, of the Hellenistic period, built by the local
architect Hermogenes. It was a building of the Ionic order
with a frieze dedicated to the War of the Amazons.

We return to Aydin and then continue to climb up the rich
valley of Büyük Menderes. At Sultanhisar we must take the
road to the left which leads to the ruins of the ancient town of
NYSA scattered amidst bushes and olive trees.

The town was founded in the 3rd century B.C. by a Seleucid
king, but it was under the Caesars that the monuments were
set up : temples, a theatre, a *bouleuterion*, etc. It was probably
abandoned during Tamerlane's conquest.

Along the rough path which leads to the theatre, we can
see vestiges of a Roman road made of large slabs of stone. We
then cross the Byzantine *enceinte* of which a few sections of
the walls remain and reach the theatre recently dug out of the
deep bed of earth which covered it. It is very well preserved.
In front of the theatre there extended a vast square laid out
above the ravine of ancient *Thymbros* and we can still see
the tunnel under which passed a conduit supplying the water
for a tank under the moving stage of the theatre where
naumachic performances were given.

Near the theatre there are eight arches belonging to a building which has not been identified.

By continuing to follow the path, we find to the right, in
an olive grove, the ruins of the *geronticon*, or Council Chamber
of the Elders, with a few rows of seats still visible. In front of
this edifice there used to be a courtyard with a fountain and
porticoes decorated in mosaic of geometric motifs, of which

one can see a few vestiges. All around lie fragments of columns, of capitals, of sculpture and of *stele* bearing inscriptions.

A little further on, on the edge of a ravine, the ruins of a pre-hellenic building can be discerned, showing the great blocks of stone and the gateway framed with moulded pillars.

But, until the monuments of Nysa are freed from the brambles and bushes which cover them, they can only offer minor interest. Notice also, 5 kilometres to the west of the site of the village of Savalatti, the former *Acharaka* where there once stood a temple set up at the entrance to a cave dedicated to Pluto and Core. A sacred way, flanked with tombs, leads to an acropolis.

We return to the highway and leave it after Kuyucak to take another rough road to the right, which leaves, on our left, the remains of *Antiochia ad Meandrum* and arrives, at the end of 23 kilometres, at the village of Geyre.

This village is modern. It was built to house the peasants whose hutments used to occupy the ancient town of *APHRODISIAS*.

This latter, situated on a plateau dominated by the Baba Dagi, and occupied since the 6th century B.C., was at all times, a city famous for its artists and was particularly brilliant during the Roman era. Caesar and Augustus took it under their protection, and the temple to Aphrodite, which had the right of asylum, attracted great crowds. The works of the sculptors of Aphrodisias were exported all over the world. The theatre, music, philosophy, rhetoric and medicine flourished and the philosopher Alexander was born there.

During the Byzantine era, the town, which was renamed *Stavropolis*—the city of the Cross—was the seat of a bishopric and, in the 4th century, the temple of Aphrodite was transformed into a church.

But the town declined from the 11th century onwards and the coming of Tamerlane completed its ruin. In the 17th century, a simple village was established on its site. Peasants

built their own hutments with ancient stones, with the shafts
of columns and they used the sarcophagi as tanks.

Now, part of the buildings which were the glory of
Aphrodisias have been unearthed and others are in course of
being excavated.

The stadium, which accommodated from 20,000 to 30,000
spectators, is perhaps the best preserved of the whole ancient
world, with its twenty-two rows of seats surmounted by a
covered promenade. This is 260 metres long, and nearly 60
metres wide.

Not far off, we can see the gymnasium and, on the other
side of the road, the temple of Aphrodite, modified into a
church, shows the alignment of its fluted columns with Ionic
capitals. We can count eight on the façade and thirteen on
the side, and it formerly housed a statue of Aphrodite nearly
3 metres high which was buried when the town became
Christian.

When the temple was transferred into a church, the walls
of the *naos* were strengthened on the outside with lateral
colonnades which formed three aisles. At the end, an apse
was constructed between the *prothesis* and the *diaconicon* and
we can still make out the presbytery with seats separated from
the outer walls by a passage decorated with frescoes. The
atrium had a fountain.

Built during the first century B.C., the temple was modified
into a church in the 4th century and, at that time, was fronted
by a narthex and an exonarthex which gave on to an open
atrium where there was also a fountain. There still remain,
in the apse, vestiges of mural paintings representing the seated
Christ and the Virgin accompanied by angels, saints, and
evangelists.

The temple of the 1st century B.C. which used to attract
crowds of pilgrims and enjoyed the rights of asylum, had
succeeded a Hellenistic sanctuary of the 3rd century B.C. This
was on a slightly different plan which itself had been preceded

by a building, either sacred or profane, of the Archaic period (7th century B.C.).

Opposite we can see the remains of a Byzantine construction probably erected under Justin II (A.D. 565–578) with materials from ancient buildings. Two capitals have been discovered where, between two branches of acanthus, the figures of Aphrodite of Cnidus and Aphrodite of Cos have been carved by Praxiteles. The building comprised a little square courtyard with two galleries with blue marble Corinthian columns which have been set up again. One of the rooms still has its marble mosaic pavement in geometric pattern. A door leads to a larger courtyard paved with marble. To the south of the basilica, a little odeon, erected towards the end of the 2nd century A.D. and reconstructed in the 4th century after an earthquake, has been excavated. By a miracle, it is intact with a dozen tiers of seats, its marble orchestra and its richly decorated stage. Behind the stage, a portico with two rows of Corinthian columns in the interior, and Ionian columns on the exterior, extends to the west and opens onto the *agora*. Other porticoes surrounded the *agora*, of which one, called the portico of Tiberius, must have been built between the years A.D. 14 and 29. Several statues decorated the portico of the *postcenium* of the odeon, notably one of a certain Alexandros Dikaios in the 3rd century A.D. To the north-west of the odeon, the ruins of the Palace of the Bishop of Caria, built in the 4th or 5th century, have been identified. This building was used, thanks to a number of restorations, right up to the 12th century. We can distinguish a triple apsidal construction, preceded by a peristyle and several rooms either paved with blue and white marble or with geometric mosaics.

The baths, with their columns, their basins, their mosaics and their underground passages, have also been excavated and marvellous sculptures with richly decorated sarcophagi have been collected together in a little temporary museum. We must notice also, beyond the temple of Aphrodite, the graceful columns of a *propylon*, either smooth or moulded, arranged in three rows and resting on high bases. The spaces between the central columns are larger, and, among the delicately carved architectural details, there is a beautiful Victory flanked by a dog and a young man, two figures of Eros and a dog running through acanthus branches.

But the city is still not entirely cleared of rubble. A graceful portico, with fluted Ionic columns, stands in a little wood of young birches and, right in the heart of the ancient village, the University of New York has uncovered the *cavea* of a theatre where the tiers of seats are carved out of the acropolis. This *cavea*, 15 metres in diameter, dominates an orchestra pit faced with marble. There is still a great mass of earth to be removed but higher up, the actual tiers, perfectly preserved, have already been cleared.

This building was covered and could, in case of need, serve as a council chamber.

Among the salvaged carvings, a relief in honour of a certain Zoilos, surrounded by allegorical figures symbolizing Valour, Honour, the City and the People, is particularly noteworthy and a most interesting example of the work of the 2nd century A.D.

Finally, the remains of an *enceinte* have been excavated. This was 3,500 metres long and covered an area of 90 hectares. It was restored between 335 and 350 when the city became Byzantine.

We must now return to the main road and if it happens to be lunchtime we can ask the young man, whom the Turkish tourist office has put at our disposal in a kiosk in the principle square of the village of Karacasu, to tell us where to find the best restaurant in the district.

We then continue towards Denizli, but just before reaching it, we take, to the left, the excellent road to PAMUKKALE which is only 20 kilometres away. As soon as we arrive there, we are confronted by an astonishing spectacle. We find ourselves

at the foot of a dazzling white cliff, forming a kind of amphitheatre. This is the result of springs of warm water saturated
with lime which flow out over a plateau of travertine and,
falling from a height of 100 metres, have left deposits of lime
on the slopes which create all sorts of basins and hollows,
spreading out like the petals of strange flowers. The water runs
in narrow trickles over the wall of rock and fills the hollows.
It is a landscape of the most astonishing beauty.

On arriving at the summit of the plateau, our attention is
arrested by two entirely different spectacles. On the one hand
a thermal establishment, bathing pools and motels ready to
welcome us, and on the other the ruins of an ancient city
which is none other than *HIERAPOLIS* founded in the 2nd
century B.C. by Eumenes II, King of Pergamum, at the time
when the Romans gave him vast territories taken from the
Seleucids after the Battle of Magnesia ad Sipylum in 190
B.C. Because of the springs giving off a great deal of carbon
which poisons the air, Hierapolis had the reputation in classical times of being one of the gates of Hades. Conquered in 88
B.C. by Mithridates Eupator, destroyed in the year A.D. 17
by an earthquake in the time of Tiberius, the city was rebuilt
and reached its height of prosperity in the 2nd and 3rd centuries. Christianity spread thanks to an important Jewish
colony and the apostle Philip was martyred there towards the
year 87. Hierapolis declined when Constantine the Great
adopted Byzantium as his capital. During the Byzantine period
it was one of the two metropolises of the Phrygian Pacatiana
and a great cathedral was built. In the 11th and 12th centuries
a fortress, of which there still subsist a few vestiges, was constructed on the side of the cliff. It was given the Turkish name
of Pamukkalesi.

On reaching the plateau, we see, to the right, the ancient
baths with a complex of rooms, of which some still have their
domes. A collection of fragments of sculpture are exhibited in
one of them.

On the way back we can see a monumental *nymphaeum*
with a fountain and semi-circular tiers of seats and the remains
of a huge basilica with three aisles, the one in the centre
terminating in a semi-circular apse. A transept enlarges the
choir which occupies the whole breadth of the church. A little
room which was perhaps a baptistery opens onto the south
transept. The church was covered with domes and, at each stage
of the central nave, massive pillars alternate with lighter ones
in the manner seen, from time to time, in our cathedrals.

This basilica may be the same cathedral we were speaking
about earlier since Hierapolis became the seat of a bishopric
in the first half of the 6th century.

The theatre, which we visit next and which backs against
the hill, is the most remarkable and the best preserved monument of Hierapolis. The *diazoma* and the corridors which give
access to it have been exposed as well as the *cavea* which had
26 rows of seats. The stage, encircled by a wall with two rows
of windows, still has important sculptured details of scrolls,
volutes, and vine branches as well as the five doors of the
façade and the two doors linking the stage with the proscenium.
The stage is cluttered up with the debris of columns and capitals
and with fragments of sculpture which used to decorate the
wall of the pulpit. These sculptures depict divinities and
allegorical figures similar to the reliefs which decorate the stage
of the theatre of Dionysos in Athens. The whole cortège of
Dionysos is represented here. These carvings have been
arranged in the little museum described earlier, but it is to be
hoped that they will be restored to their original position.

If we climb up above the theatre, we shall find the remains
of the ramparts flanked with heavy square bastions and, on the
outside of the walls, to the north-east, on a terrace, the remains
of a Byzantine church with an octagonal sanctuary. This may
well have been the martyrium of St. Philip the Evangelist,
martyred on this spot with his two daughters, Hermione and
Eutyches, and his two sons.

The sanctuary was composed of a great central octagon inscribed in a vast square 60 metres in area with four straight corridors along the side. Eight radiating rectangular chapels were separated by a number of polygonal rooms provided with three niches. In the centre of each of the four corridors, a little door led into a small, square, domed room serving as a narthex. We can enter one of the eight chapels and from there get in to the octagonal room. We can also get, from the radiating chapels by means of passages cut into the corridor, in to the polygonal rooms on seven sides which are situated in the alignment of the main columns of the octagon. The little rooms with three apses were lighted by small courtyards which also illuminated the rectangular chapels in the diagonals of the octagon.

The central hall, which was 20·73 metres in diameter, was covered with a dome with wooden ribs faced on the outside with lead sheets. The radiating arms were covered with cupolas of brick whilst the rooms between these arms were only covered with wood, with the exception of the terminal apses which were surmounted with half-domes faced with mosaic. At least two of the four corridors which surrounded the building were lined with porticoes.

We now turn our steps towards the principal gate of Hierapolis which can be seen in the distance by following an old canal bed filled up with lime deposits. This enables us to cross the site of the ruins which extend between the baths and the gate and to pass in front of the remains of a vast basilica with three aisles separated by marble columns. The main apse still has the steps of a *synthronon* where the members of the clergy sat during services. Then, when this church was already in ruins, a short while before the abandonment of the city, a little church with a single nave was constructed upon the site of the southern wing.

Further on, we shall pass a gate of the Byzantine era. On this side the rampart is in a good state of preservation. We then

follow a strip of the ancient road which crosses a block of houses
of the Roman era. In Byzantine times the level of the fairway
was raised and its width reduced.

We finally arrive at a monumental gateway which was
doubtless erected by Julius Frontinus, proconsul of Asia, in A.D.
82–83. Near this gate, with three entrances opening between
two round towers, we should notice against the southern tower
a *hypogeum*, originally isolated but which was incorporated in
the town during the time of its development in the Domitian
period. This *hypogeum*, rectangular in plan, was faced with
slabs of marble and preceded by a portico.

Beyond the gate, can be seen the imposing structure of an
ancient thermal establishment which was modified into a
church at the beginning of the Byzantine era.

Further still stands one of the best preserved necropoles of
Asia Minor. The tombs are dispersed along the two sides of
the path which goes towards Tripolis and Ephesus.

There are a large variety of tombs, dating from the tumuli
of the Hellenistic period or the time of Augustus, which enclose
a funerary chamber, circular in plan on the exterior, to the
simple sarcophagi, and also *hypogea* with sloping roofs and
pediments. A number of tombs have been re-erected as well
as a little *exedra* with a stone bench.

On the way back we can follow along the cliff so as to get a
better view of the encrustations which seem to be embroidered
over the slopes, and this also gives us a chance to pass near the
remains of a little fortress of the 11th century in the interior
of which has been installed a Tusan Hotel.

Returning to Denizli, five kilometres after reaching the road
we have just left, we can veer to the right in order to see on
an arid plateau the ruins of ancient *Laodicea* founded in the
3rd century B.C. by Antiochus II on or near the site of an even
more ancient city which, according to Pliny the Younger, was
called *Dispolis*. The new town took the name of *Laodicea ad
Lycum*.

After the defeat of the Seleucids at the Battle of Magnesia
ad Sipylum in 190 B.C., the Romans allotted Laodicea to their
ally, the King of Pergamum. On the death of Attalus III in 133
B.C., a Roman garrison occupied the town which in 88 B.C.
suffered a siege by Mithridates, King of Pontus, who took
possession of it and held it until the year 84 B.C. After an
earthquake in the 1st century of our era, decay set in, but it
was reconstructed and the Emperor Commodus (180–192)
conferred on it the title of *Neocore*. It included an important
Jewish colony which was early converted to Christianity and
became one of the seven churches of the Apocalypse. Ravaged
in 1097 by a Seleucid invasion, it was retaken by the Byzantines but, at the end of the 13th century, the Turks seized it
and the inhabitants gradually abandoned it and installed themselves in Denizli.

We therefore see a vast desert in front of us; a plateau
intersected by ravines where sections of walls and half-buried
arcades emerge from the mass of rubble. Until systematic
excavation is put into operation, any impression of these ruins
is disappointing.

Notice the remains of a Roman aqueduct and, further on,
those of a bridge over which the road to Ephesus used to run.

We finally arrive at DENIZLI which was very much
damaged in 1710 by an earthquake, followed by a fire. After
this, the new town was reconstructed outside the original walls.
There is nothing here of real interest except a bazaar founded
in the 11th century in a fortified enclosure.

We now take the road to Burdur, and after 8 kilometres
reach the Seleucid caravanserai of AK HAN, built in the
13th century. Rectangular in plan, it comprises a square interior
court, with porticoes on two sides and a domed hall resting on
two rows of three pillars. The beautiful gateway to the great
hall of the caravanserai bears a sculptured inscription attribut-
ing to Karasungur in the reign of the Sultan Kaykavus the
completion of this part of the Han on 23 September 1253.

The rest of the caravanserai was probably finished in 1254.

The mosque must have been situated on the first floor in the left corner at the back of the court because what seems to be a bath was found to the right of the entrance.

Our rather monotonous route now goes through Bozkurt and at Cardak passes over several level crossings. Near Cardak we can see to the left of the railway, the ruins of another caravanserai dated 1230 of which there remains a large vaulted hall with five aisles.

We then see, to the right, Aci Gölü, the ancient *Lake Sanaos* on the banks of which we shall find the ancient town of the same name.

We leave, to the left, the road to Dinar which has nothing of interest to offer, and further on to the right, the road to Burdur. In continuing towards Konya, we must take the road to Isparta.

ISPARTA, which occupies the site of the old Byzantine town of *Baris*, at the foot of Mount Ağlasun, with its little white houses, has a most picturesque aspect, situated in a fertile plain famous for its fields of roses, but there is no monument of interest and the citadel is completely in ruins.

Twenty kilometres further on, we see on our left, a solitary minaret then we go over a pass, from which we reach the lake and the town of Egridir.

EGRIDIR is a pleasant little city on a promontory forming a peninsula into the lake. It is the former Byzantine town of *Prostanna*. In the 13th century it formed part of the estate of the Sultan of Roum. It was the most important town of the region.

The Emir Felekeddin Dündar, who gave it the name of *Felekabad,* installed himself there, abandoning the earlier capital of Uluborlu, but, with the unification of Turkey, the town lost its importance as a fortress.

Of the remains left by the Seljuks, we can see the Dundär

1. APHRODISIAS : TEMPLE OF APHRODITE

4. ESKI GUMÜS

Medresesi, formerly a caravanserai with a beautiful stalactite gateway, which was succeeded by Ulu Camii, the Great Mosque erected in the 15th century and the ancient wall which barred the entrance to the peninsula. It is to be regretted that the gate, which is particularly imposing with its two different towers, is disfigured by a hotel which has been built just in front of it, as well, needless to say, as the usual electric pylons.

But we shall find it very pleasant to stroll through the lanes of the old town with their picturesque houses of stone and wood, and the two rocky islands which prolong the point and were originally joined to the land and inhabited until recently by a Greek community.

The site of ancient *Prostanna* lies at the top of Davras Daği which dominates the lake. During the Byzantine area, it was the seat of a bishopric. The town spread over a depression which links the Davras Daği to another point. It still subsists at the top of the acropolis as well as a very much ruined *enceinte* and the remains of what may have been a temple.

Our way now goes along the lake of Egridir, with beautiful views across the water and the mountains which surround it. After about 30 kilometres we see, to the left, the caravanserai of Ertokus, constructed in 1213 or 1223, where a beautiful gateway, with panels in two colours, leads to the main hall.

We then leave to the left, the road for Yalvaç, a great township situated near the ruins of *ANTIOCHIA IN PISIDIA*.

The town, according to Strabo, may have been founded on the southern slope of the mountain which separates Pisidia from Phrygia by Seleucus Nicator, a little before 280 B.C. After the defeat of Antiochus III in 190 B.C. at the battle of Magnesia ad Sipylum, Antioch was declared a free city. At the death of king Amyntas, the town reverted to Rome and Augustus sent his lieutenant, Publius Sulpicius Quirinus, to pacify the region and to confer concessions on the city. In the course of their

c

journeys, St. Paul and St. Barnabas sojourned in Antioch which was very prosperous during the Roman era. It was almost certainly destroyed in A.D. 713 during an Arab invasion.

The ruins of the old town are 2 kilometres from the township, itself situated on the right bank of the former river Anthios which flows across a deep gorge to the east of the acropolis of Antioch. Excavations have unearthed several buildings, especially the remains of the *propylaea* of the acropolis with triple arches in the Corinthian style, which date from the restoration of the town by Augustus.

From the *propylaea* we reach a square, called the Augustus Platea, which ends in a semi-circular esplanade reached through a double portico, Ionic on the ground level and Doric on the first storey. In the axis of this square there used to be a temple erected in honour of Augustus.

Another square in front of the *propylaea*, called Tiberia Platea, in honour of Tiberius, was lined along the north side with booths beneath a portico. We can still make out in the ground the markings for games such as knuckle bones. In a corner there are vestiges of a round building set up by Marcus Aurelius.

A little to the west, the remains of a cruciform Byzantine church have been found and, more to the north, another basilica with a mosaic pavement. One inscription bears the name of Optimus, the bishop of Antiochia in Pisidia (A.D. 375–381).

In order to reach Konya we must be careful not to take the Beysehir road; we should go straight towards Akşehir, a route which crosses the imposing bare mountain range. Without being good, the road is quite negotiable and at Akşehir we return to the surfaced highway from Afyon to Konya.

AKŞEHIR is a very lively little town on the site of the old Byzantine city of *Philomenion*, which was taken by the Turks towards the end of the 11th century. The famous satirical writer, Nasrettin Hoca, was born there in the 14th century and his *türbe*, is the most interesting monument in the town. It is very simple in design with six pillars supporting a dome.

The *türbe* stands in the middle of a beautiful garden. We can still see the ruins of the Tas Medrese built in stone by Keykavus I in 1216 with stones from antique buildings, and the *türbe* of Sayyid Mahmud of 1224.

The road to Konya follows a straight line across the steppe, passing through Ilgin, a township famous from classical times for its thermal springs, and Kadinhanli where we can see, to the right of the road, a Seljuk caravanserai built in 1223. The great vaulted hall is well preserved. We can distinguish material from buildings used in a funerary *stele*, and the niche of a *mirhab* of restrained decoration in the little mosque of the *han*.

Another caravanserai, the Haç Hafiz, 20 kilometres further on to the left, dates from the 19th century. It replaced another caravanserai of the 13th century of which we can make out a few vestiges.

We return to the road from Ankara to Konya which we soon reach.

KONYA, situated in the middle of the sunbaked steppe, is a veritable oasis of gardens and orchards watered by abundant streams. The origins of the town go back to the 3rd millenium, but the town we see rebuilt is a Phrygian city which, ravaged during the 7th century, came under the successive rule of the Lydians, the Persians, the Seleucid kings, of Pergamum, then of the Romans. Known under the name of *Iconium*, it took that of *Claudiconimum* in honour of Claudius. St. Paul and St. Barnabus sojourned here on several occasions. But Konya is pre-eminently the capital of the Seljuk sultans and it became filled with monuments from the reign of Ala et Tin Kaykobat at the beginning of the 13th century. His successors also built there. It was during the 13th century, too, that the famous poet and mystic, Celal et Tin Rumi, founded a monastery of Dervishes here whose influence spread throughout Islam.

Enlightened sultans became great developers, patrons of the arts and able administrators.

We next leave the government quarter surrounded by modern administrative buildings, and follow the Ala et Tin Bulvari which leads us to the Ala et Tin Park.

On arrival we see several mosques. To begin with, the *Seref et Tin Camii*, a huge mosque in the Ottoman style built in 1636 and restored in 1853. Then there is the *Iplikçi Camii* built at the beginning of the 13th century by the Grand Vizir Sems et Tin but recently restored. It is mainly interesting for its stalactite *mihrab* where we can see glazed tiles of the beginning of the 13th century.

We then arrive at a great circular space with a mound in the centre on which used to stand the ancient Seljuk citadel and which is surmounted by the *Ala et Tin Camii*. This mosque, begun in the reign of Sultan Masut I and completed by Ala et Tin Kaykobat in 1220, was the work of the architect Mohammad ben Khaulan who was a native of Damascus which explains why the mosque is in the Seljuk Damascan style.

In the prayer hall, the forty-two antique columns with Roman and Byzantine capitals support a wooden roof. The *mimber* dates from 1156 and is doubtless the oldest known example. Its delicate arabesques constitute a masterpiece of wood carving. The *mirhab* has been carried out in painted plaster and different coloured marbles.

The adjacent *türbe* was erected by Kilic Arsian II (1155–1192) on an octagonal plan with a pyramid roof. Five of the ten cenotaphs it encloses are of Seljuk Sultans.

One of the two others *türbes* in the court of the mosque was built in the reign of Ala et Tin Kaykobat by the Syrian architect Yusuf ibn Abd el Ghaffar. It is reached through the prayer hall, and the sultan had his ancestors' remains placed here.

The mosque used to be inside the citadel; the ramparts have

disappeared, as well as the palace built in 1220 by Ala et Tin Kaykobat.

We shall next look at the remarkable monuments that surround the square. First there is the *Büyük Karatay Medresi*, former college of Koranic theology, built in 1251 by the Emir Celal et Tin Karatay. Its magnificent marble portal is richly decorated with interlacing, stalactites and twisted columns. It was inspired by the monumental entrance to the mosque which we have just seen, and its architect from Damascus has once again brought to Anatolia the sober Syrian architecture with its knots of ribbons and its two half-arches interlocked.

From here we can enter the courtyard where the students used to lodge in little cells, and then go into the Great Hall with a dome, where the four pendentives, ornamented with glazed mosaic, balance the square plan of the hall. At the base of the dome, a band of faience runs round the drum. Here is endlessly repeated in Kufic characters the Surat el Fath (Victory).

The *Karatay Medrese*, which has been turned into a museum of Ceramics has a remarkable collection of fragments from all periods. We can also visit an *iwan* and a *türbe* where more glazed faience is displayed.

If we continue to follow round the citadel mound, we shall come to the *Ince Minare Medresesi* with a portal which is no less impressive. This little Seljuk medrese was built by the vizier Sahip Atâ Fahr et Tin Ali in 1265 for the teaching of the "Hadith". His architect, Kaloub Abdullah, designed a building very similar in style—the mosque of Sahib Atâ, built in 1258, which we shall see later. It is an architectural achievement of astonishing originality with its predominance of vertical lines, its broad epigraphic bands, its columns, its knots and palm leaves which cover the whole façade.

The minaret beside the building was partly destroyed by lightning in 1901 so that the name of Ince Minaret (slender minaret) is no longer appropriate.

The interior houses a museum of sculpture in wood and in stone of the Seljuk period; bas reliefs, mosque doorways, lecterns, etc.

The plan is similar to that of the Karatay Medresi except that there are no cells at the entrance, only a little square vestibule.

If we continue towards the right we shall reach the *Sirçali Medresesi*, a former college of Koranic theology built in 1242 by the Seljuk vizier, Bedr et Tin Muslih. It contains a museum of funerary monuments.

Without being as sumptuous as the former ones we have seen, the portal, with its deep niche, is amply decorated. The *türbe* of the founder is to the right of the entrance and, on the other side of the courtyard where the Koran was taught in the summer, is an *iwân* which has in part preserved its remarkable glazed faience decorations.

These mosaics, superbly handled and incomparably majestic, are a very high achievement in this art of geometric and calligraphic decoration. They bear the signature of a certain Mohammed, son of Mohammed, son of Othman, a builder of Tous (Eastern Iran) and this inscription : "I have created these decorations which have no parallel in the world. I shall perish, but they will remain as a memorial to me."

The next lane we come to leads to the *Habey dar ül Huffaz*, formerly a hospice built in 1421 during Karamanid times. The walls of brick are faced with carved marble slabs. The dome is supported by a polygonal drum with sixteen faces attached to the base by triangular pyramids. The bricks which surround the dome seem to indicate that others had been super-imposed.

The polylobed arch of the gate is of oriental inspiration.

The end of the road which we have just followed leads into the *Sahip Atâ Camii*, a Seljuk mosque erected in 1269 by the *vizier*, Sahip Atâ Fahr et Tin Ali.

As we have already noted, it is the work of the same archi-

tect who constructed the Ince Minareli Medrese, and its portal
is also very richly ornamented with a stalactite niche above the
entrance and four windows. The lower ones serve as fountains.
The minaret has a fluted stem, and the folding door belongs
to the Seljuk period.

The mosque was partly destroyed, but we can still see in the
prayer hall the *mimber* and a very beautiful *mirhab* with
stalactites decorated with glazed faience.

There is also an oratory, a *hammam* and a *türbe*, decorated
with glazed tiles, where the founder is interred. .

Nearby in the archaeological museum there is a very beautiful sarcophagus of the middle of the 3rd century A.D., Sidi-
maran in type and decorated with bas-reliefs of the Labours of
Hercules.

There still remains to be seen at the other end of the town,
another complex formed by the tomb of Mevlâna and the
Selimiye Camii. This latter, the mosque of Selim II, was erected
between 1566 and 1574 in the style of the great mosques of
the sultans of Sinan. It is preceded by a portico with six columns
with polychrome arches covered with little cupolas. The square
prayer hall is surmounted by a large dome. The *mimber* is
faced with polychrome marble.

The Tekke of Mevlâna which completely fills the end of the
square, is an ancient monastery of Dancing Dervishes founded
in the 13th century by Mevlâna Cella et Tin Rumi and now
transformed into an Islamic museum. Inside the entrance gate
there is a courtyard paved with marble with a marble fountain
with a roof supported by graceful colonettes as well as several
little *türbes* of the 16th century.

From the vestibule we can enter into a Great Hall where
there is a collection of carpets, illuminated manuscripts and
several cenotaphs, then we come to the *türbe* of Mevlâna, the
only building of the 13th century. It is surmounted by a ribbed
tower covered with green glazed faience. The remains of the
founder of the Order of Dancing Dervishes rest in a marble

sarcophagus covered with brocade and surrounded by a wrought silver grille in 1599.

We can then visit the former dancing room of the Dervishes where some extraordinary musical instruments are exhibited and, in other rooms, some ancient Korans, very old prayer rugs etc.

Finally we must go and see, 8 kilometres away over an excellent road, the little town of SILLE with its catacombs and its Byzantine churches.

We have to stop in the middle of the village to get the key to the old Byzantine church which is on the other side of the river at the foot of a mountain out of which troglodyte dwellings have been hollowed. This little church, which has been completely spoiled inside, still has some beautiful window surrounds and a central dome.

The rupestral churches have some remains of frescoes and we have a foretaste of what awaits us in Cappadocia.

Those who are making for Antalya should continue towards BURDUR instead of taking the Isparta road. Burdur is the ancient *Arkania Limnae*. It is now a lively little town where there is not much to see except the *Ulu Camii*, built in the 14th century by Dündar Bey, and the archaeological museum which contains inscriptions and sculpture from sites in the region, particularly some reliefs of the Pisidian god, Kakasbos.

We should notice 45 kilometres further on, 2 kilometres to the right of the highway, the remains of a Seljuk caravanserai of the 13th century known by the name of *Incir Han*. There is practically nothing left except a great hall with a door with a multifoil arch and geometric motifs as well as two reliefs of lions. A little further on, a road to the left leads to Bucak, 3 kilometres away, and to Melli which is 29 kilometres distant.

From Bucak it takes two hours and a half to walk to ancient *Hyia* of which only a scrap of the polygonal masonry of a wall remains and a few niches that belonged to a sanctuary.

The site of *Milyas* has been located at about a kilometre from
Melli. At the summit of the hill there remain some portions of
a rampart in polygonal masonry dating from the beginning of
the Hellenistic era and, on the slope, a theatre of which about
a dozen stone tiers remain. Near the theatre are vestiges of an
important building with a façade with seven doors and, further
on, groups of ruined buildings. The main necropolis shows a
number of sarcophagi and funerary monuments. On the road
from Melli we pass near a hill on the slope of which we can
see a rupestral carving.

A third, but unidentified, ancient city is to be found 20
kilometres to the west of the fork, three hours on horseback
from the village of Kestel. The remains of fortifications and
buildings, of which a sanctuary dedicated to Pluto and Kore, a
rupstral relief, etc., have been located.

A kilometre to the left of the road near the village of Susuz,
a caravanserai was erected a little before 1246, but nothing
remains save the great hall with a beautiful portal with geometric motifs and a vault decorated with stalactites. The dome
of the hall is in a good state of preservation.

We then continue to Dağ, a little hamlet at the foot of the
pass of Çubuk from which we can reach the village of Karaot,
15 kilometres away. An hour and a half's walk from here lies
the site of *Osai*, or *Sia*, of which there subsists some polygonal
masonry of a reasonably well preserved rampart with a gate
at the top of the hill on which the city stood. The ruins of
a theatre or a *bouleuterion* can be seen on the slope and, down
below this, a necropolis.

At the end of the Gorge of Çubuk, 300 metres to the left
of the road, was the *Caravanserai of Kirkgöz* built between
1236 and 1246 in the reign of Kayhosrow II.

We reach it through an undecorated vaulted portal which
leads to a courtyard with rooms along the sides. Opposite is
the vaulted main hall which has seven bays.

We go over the pass of Çubuk, 875 metres high, and the road

then descends to the plain of Pamphylia, with numerous and often dangerous hairpin bends.

Near the village of Yeşilbayir, 2 kilometres away from the road to the right, are the ruins of an ancient site not far from those of a caravanserai known as *Evdir Han*.

The entrance to the caravanserai is through a beautiful portal with stalactite decoration and the courtyard is surrounded with porticoes under which there used to be rooms.

We now regain the road to Fethiye and those who had to abandon following it from Fethiye to Antalya because of its bad state can at least go and see the ruins of *TERMESSOS*, as those are only 20 kilometres away.

Termessos of Pamphylia, on its extraordinary site and with its relatively well preserved buildings, has been described in Itinerary VIII, (Vol. 1).

We rejoin the route to Antalya.

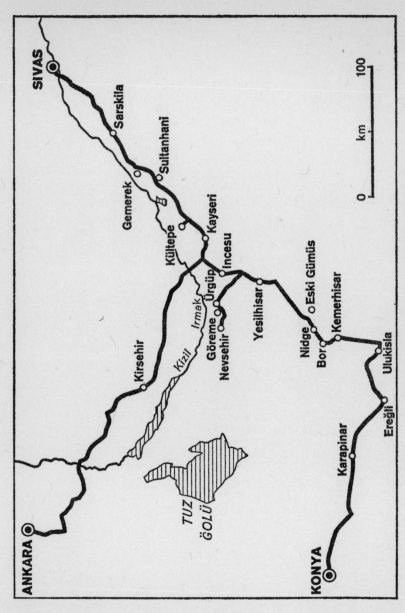

FROM KONYA TO KAYSERI, ANKARA AND SIVAS

ITINERARY II

FROM KONYA TO KAYSERI, SIVAS AND ANKARA

*Eregli — Nigde — Yesilhisar — Ürgüp — Ortahisar
— Avcilar — Nevsehir — Avanos — Göreme —
Kayseri — Kirsehir — Ankara — Kültepe —
Sultanhani — Sivas*

ON this itinerary we shall explore the strange and marvellous countryside of Cappadocia which we will find around Ürgüp and Nevsehir before reaching Kayseri. We notice to the left the curious crater lake of Karapinar and, after 145 kilometres, we leaves to the right the road to EREGLI which is only 3 kilometres away. This is *Heraclea of Cappadocia* of classical times which was captured by the Arabs in 806 in spite of its heavy fortifications. In 1101 two columns of Crusaders, who were heading towards the Holy Land after the passage of the first Crusade, had been defeated there by the Turks near the town. This latter was taken in 1211 by the troops of Leo II, king of Silesian Armenia. Towards the middle of the 13th century it came into the hands of the Mongols who were supplanted in 1467 by the Karamanoglu.

The town today has nothing to offer of interest but it is possible, with a certain amount of difficulty, to see a rupestral bas-relief 17 kilometres away near the village of Ivriz. It was carried out by a king Tuvanova, contemporary of Tiglath Pileser III (745–722 B.C.), king of Assyria. It represents a lion whose name, Tarhun, is known to us, thanks to three passages of hieroglyphics. He is crowned with a tiara of horns, holding a handful of maize in his left hand and a vine plant in his right hand, whilst, in front of him, the king, in an attitude of respect, is clothed in an Assyrian tunic with richly embroidered border. The boots, with pointed turned up toes, are like those one sees in Hittite bas-reliefs.

Further on, we regain the highway which comes from Ankara. We go over a pass 1460 metres high and through the village of ULUKIŞLA which owes its name, the great barracks, to a 17th-century caravanserai which we can see to the left. We then leave the road to Adana to the right, to take the one to Nigde.

Fifty kilometres further on, we leave, to the left, the road to Bor which goes through the little village of KEMERHISAR 4 kilometres away, situated near the site of ancient *Tyana* of which there are only insignificant remains.

Tyana may be none other than the ancient Hittite town of Tuvanova founded before the arrival of the Hittites in Asia Minor. Conquered by Labarna, who made one of his sons governor, it seems to have been the principle centre of the cult devoted to the god Vurunkatti, a Hittite divinity identified with the Sumerian god, Zababa. Here they also used to venerate Teshub, god of storms, represented stabbing a bull. At the beginning of the 14th century B.C., Tuvanova was invaded by the people of Arzawa, but they were forced back by Suppiluliuma I. After the destruction of the new Hittite empire of Anatolia towards 1200, Tuvanova became one of the prin- ciple towns of the neo-Hittite state of Tabal which resisted Assyrian pressure up to the 7th century B.C.

In Roman and Byzantine times, *Tyana* became a stronghold which resisted Arab power right up to the 8th century A.D. but, taken by surprise and pillaged, it gradually declined and was abandoned in favour of Bor and Nigde towards the end of the 11th century.

BOR has only limited interest—a *bedestan* of the 15th or

16th century and a *hamman* of the Ottoman period which is
alongside.

It is preferable, then, to take the direct route for NIGDE
which we reach after crossing a fertile plain planted with
orchards. The town is spread out at the foot of a hill crowned
with the remains of an old fortress. This latter, which we reach
after having left, to the right, the Hamman Camii, a little
mosque where we shall find two antique columns, was founded
towards the end of the 11th century by the Seljuk Sultan, Ala
et Tin, then restored towards 1470 by Isak Pasha who was no
doubt responsible for the beautiful polygonal keep which is still
standing. Of the wall reinforced with bastions which surrounds
the mound, there remain the entrance to the fortress and
sections of curtain with two rectangular towers transformed
into houses.

Near to this, the *Ala et Tin Camii*, the most beautiful of the
mosques of the town, has recently been disaffected and restored.
Above a sumptuous portal decorated with arabesques, an
inscription affirms that the sanctuary was erected in 1203 by
Besares, son of Abdullah Zein et Tin, former governor of Nigde
in the reign of Kaykavus, then restored by Ala et Tin.

The façade, with courses of grey and yellow stone, is flanked
by a cylindrical minaret on an octagonal substructure with a
stalactite cornice. The prayer hall has three aisles separated
by two rows of four columns, those at the end being covered
with domes. The *mihrab* is formed by a vaulted niche with
stalactites set up in a larger alcove framed with a border of
geometric design.

Behind and below the mosque, the *bedestan*, built in the 16th
or 17th century, looks like a vaulted street flanked with shops.
Three gates with dropped arches, give access to it.

In the little square in front of the *bedestan*, at the foot of
the citadel, stands the *Sungur Bey Camii* which was erected in
the first quarter of the 14th century by the chief of a Mongol
tribe. Access is from the north side by a beautiful portal with

many panels in geometric designs and graceful mouldings. Another portal, no less richly decorated, opening to the east, also gives access to the prayer hall. Above its lintel made of curved keystones beautifully faced, we can see a partly ruined rose window which gives a Gothic appearance to this entrance.

The prayer hall, very much restored after a fire in the 18th century, has five aisles, though it only had three originally. A pulpit was built on the north side and is illuminated by two rectangular windows surmounted by little rose windows. The *mihrab* is surrounded by sculptured decorations, and a little door opens into an octagonal *türbe*, doubtless intended for Sungur Bey, but empty.

This mosque presents a curious mixture of Islamic elements and elements inspired by western art like the capitals, the ogival vaults and the rose windows, and this would imply the presence of Christian artists from Cyprus.

We must not miss the *Eskiciler Çeşmeşi fountain* erected in 1421 and behind it the *Şah Mesçiti*, a little oratory of the 15th century in which there are a few columns and re-used Byzantine capitals.

By taking a lane from the square to the left of the Sungur Bey Camii, we can reach the *Ak Medrese* which houses an archaeological museum.

The white *medrese* is an excellent example of a two storey building of this kind, it was built in 1409. We enter through a magnificent portal with a honeycomb niche and delicately carved arabesque decoration.

The courtyard is lined with two rows of porticoes with arcades in tiercepoint, through which we can enter the theological students' rooms except to the south where there is a large *iwân* provided with a *mihrab*.

Next we come to the *Diş Cami*, a little Ottoman mosque built in the 16th century in which the beautiful *mimber* of carved wood encrusted with mother-of-pearl comes from the Sungur Bey Camii.

All that is left to see now is the three *türbes* of which the
most beautiful is certainly the most original and the most
remarkable monument of Nigde. It is the *Hudavent Türbesi*
built in 1312 for princess Hudavent Hatun, daughter of Sultan
Rükn et Tin Kilic Arslan IV who was interred there in 1331.
This mausoleum is set up on an octagonal base, but thanks
to cornices decorated with stalactites it becomes a polygonal
with sixteen faces. Under the short cornice is a strip of writing
on white marble, whilst the framing of the doors and windows
are also in marble with extraordinarily rich decoration. The
portal, flanked by two little columns surmounted by a broken
arch, has above the niche of the door an inscription which
mentions the name of the princess. There are windows like those
in the funerary chamber. They are surmounted with several
bas-reliefs representing a lion, birds of prey with outstretched
wings, birds with human heads, etc. Each of the sixteen faces
of the upper part is decorated with an arch where the tympanum is adorned with floral reliefs. The pyramid roof crowns
a dome on supports. In the inside there is a little *mihrab* with
a niche decorated with stalactites.

The second *türbe* dates from the beginning of the 14th
century and the third which is half destroyed from 1324.

We must leave Nigde by the route to Mayseri, but after 7
kilometres a road to the right leads to Gümüs and Eski
Gümüs, two villages which are only a kilometre away and
separated by a ravine. It is in the second village that we
shall see the magnificent rupestral church of ESKI
GÜMÜS.

A passage cut into the rock leads to a courtyard, also
hollowed out of the rock. The façade in front of us is decorated
with arches carved in the rocky mass and pierced with several
openings. To the left we find the exonarthex and, to the right,
a passage leading to a narthex with a barrel vault and decorated
with paintings. We notice particularly, to the left of the
entrance, a Virgin and Child between the archangels Michael

D

and Gabriel. From the narthex we enter into the church, also cut into the rock; square in plan, it has a dome resting on four great columns and a large apse. In the wall to the left, a great alcove contains two sarcophygi, whilst a passage leads to a little funerary chamber with an apse. We should notice, in the middle of the north wall, a well-conceived *Annunciation and a Nativity*. In the central apse, there are three rows of paintings. The *Christ Pantocrator*, in the centre of the dome, with the *Virgin*, *St. Michael* and the *Symbols of St. Matthew and of St. Luke*, to the left, and *St. John the Baptist*, to the right. The rest of the composition has disappeared. We can make out, in the central strip, the *Apostles* and the *Evangelists* and, in the lower section, the *Virgin* at prayer with elders of the church. These paintings seem to belong to two different periods of the 11th century. The paintings we have just mentioned belong to the second period.

We go back to the highway to Kayseri which crosses the steppe and has nothing of interest for us. Nevertheless, we should notice 10 kilometres further on, to the right of the road, and a certain distance away, the isolated Basilica of ESKI ANDA-VAL which some have attributed to Constantine, but is not earlier than the 6th century. It is reduced to a central nave with a polygonal apse on the outside; fragments of frescoes, black and very faded, can still be seen on the dome and doubtless dates back to the first iconoclastic period.

We then pass near the ruins of Misli Hani and Hüyük Hani, both to the right; then we leave a track, also on the right, for Çarikli and Dikilitas (or Enegli) where there is a Roman column and the ruins of the Basilica of St. Pacomos of 660, which may be the oldest example of the Cappadocian type of horseshoe apse. We go through Yeşilihisar, a large village without any interest, and then take, to the left, the road to Ürgüp, which crosses over a vast chain of bare mountains and will lead us into the heart of Cappadocia where the astonishing lands-cape and rupestral churches form one of the major curiosities

of Turkey and count among the strangest and most unbeliev-
able things to be seen in the world.

As though by magic the waters and the winds have created
in the particularly soft volcanic tufa of this region twisted forms
which mainly take on the semblance of cones. They are sometimes isolated or huddled against each other; some of them are
surmounted by a harder rock which has resisted erosion. These
are capped pyramids or the "chimneys of the fairies". They
evoke lunar landscapes since there is nothing here resembling
any of the familiar forms on our planet, although they are
inserted, from time to time, in stretches of cultivated land and
in fertile valleys which contrast with the bare, desert-like
appearance of the whole landscape. Villages appear, here and
there, round the cones or in the cones themselves; some very
imposing, already playing the role of fortresses, since the
Christian population sought refuge here at the time of the first
Arab invasions from the 7th century, but it is possible that these
isolated places may have, before that time, attracted Cenobites
as in the Thebaïde of Egypt; and there may already have been,
in the days of St. Basil the Great, religious communities established in troglodyte monasteries. On the other hand, traces
have been found of Armenian colonies who may have been
installed in Cappadocia during the 10th and 11th centuries.

As far as the rupestral churches and monasteries are concerned, if certain of them are even earlier, their painted decorations were not executed before the 9th century which was the
most creative period in religious art. Most of them date from the
10th and 11th centuries when peace was re-established under
the Macedonian Dynasty. In some cases, inscriptions give
precise details of dates of execution and of the personalities of
the donors. They come from the first half of the 10th century
to the end of the 13th century. The style of these frescoes is
more similar to the art of Syria than to the art of Constantinople. Pictorially they are very strange, for they sometimes
take the form of rows of continuous friezes displayed in parallel

strips as if to recount an entire story. They are in a primitive style with harsh angular lines, the colour applied in separate patches and the characters crowded one against another. From the end of the 10th century, contacts with Constantinople were more frequent. Church architecture became more sophisticated and the themes of the frescoes were the same as those employed in the metropolis; the colours were more varied and the attitudes more dramatic.

We go over the pass of Karacavarin, 1,535 metres high, and through the little village of Demirtis against a cliff to the right of the road. We can see, to the left, the first cones which give the strange character to the countryside of Cappadocia, then, to the right, the valley of Boyali which we shall describe on the return journey.

We now arrive at ÜRGÜP which is a good centre for exploring Cappadocia. Ürgüp was a quite important town in Byzantine times, particularly in the 10th and 11th centuries. It is situated on the edge of a amphitheatre which opens out towards the valley of Kizil Irmak at the foot of a cliff carved out with rupestral dwellings and we can see there some rather lovely houses entirely in the spirit of Byzantium with loggias and gracefully carved decorative battlements. Ürgüp was the seat of the Bishop of Haghios Prokopios who is mentioned for the first time in the records of the Emperor Leon VI (888–912) but disappears in the records of John Tzimisces (969–976).

Ürgüp is the point of departure for an excursion in Cappadocia which can be completed in a single day through roads which are mostly well-surfaced and which we shall begin by describing. There is a new hotel which is very much more comfortable and much better situated at Uçhisar and built in a regional style. It is well worth while making a stay here so as to explore this fascinating region more thoroughly.

We must leave Ürgüp by the road to Nevsehir which climbs to the heights of the upper town and goes through a passage cut out of the tufa giving us a chance to see, to the right, a first dreamlike landscape with a whole assembly of cones with some in the foreground crowned with natural capitals of hard rock.

We take, to the left, the road for ORTAHISAR, a little village with the houses crowded round an enormous rock riddled with troglodyte dwellings, looking just like a fortress which, in fact, it was. We shall go through the town where the minaret of a mosque rises up beside the rock and we descend just as far as the bridge on a lower level from which we shall have an absolutely astonishing view of this whole complex of semi-cave dwellings on the slope.

We return to the highway to Nevsehir which we leave to continue towards Aksarak so as to see 20 kilometres away, near KAY MAKLI, a recently discovered subterranean troglodyte city. Cut out of the rock, it would seem, between the 6th and the 10th centuries, it has eight floors of cells and galleries. One other subterranean town, DERINKUYU, is no less astonishing with its church reached by climbing down 35 steps.

The entire population of the village could live in this manner underground, safe from Arab invasions; the underground town, being invisible and passed over by the invaders and, moreover, just as easy to defend as the eagles' nests transformed into fortresses and dwellings. The principle entrances were barred by huge slabs of stone.

We come back to Nevsehir which we do not visit. It offers nothing of particular interest and, in contrast to what happens in other villages, where the peasants and the children pleasantly offer you whatever they have with open hands, the children here are inclined to throw stones at motorists.

We take the road to ÜÇHISAR which is, without any doubt, the most extraordinary of all the villages of Cappadocia. A comfortable hotel has just been opened where, among other amenities, two taps in each room provide the white or the red wine of the country which is excellent. From this hotel, there is also a superb view across an utterly fantastic landscape.

Like Ortahisar, Üçhisar has an enormous tufa peak which forms a real stronghold. Around this peak rise up dozens of cones with troglodyte dwellings which take on the appearance of grotesque faces with fantastic hats such as Heironymus Bosch painted. These houses, which are not cut out of the rock, are very pleasantly decorated with carvings. The population is amiable and willing; the children offer you fruit; the women gathered around the hearth where they are baking their cakes, hasten to offer one to each traveller. To refuse them or to attempt to pay is considered an insult.

By taking the route to Avcilar we shall find another series of cones and peaks of very striking shapes. In one of these cones to the right of the road a rupestral church has been discovered.

AVCILAR is a picturesque village partly troglodyte. One of the cones has a façade with two columns cut into the rock in the manner of antique tombs. We will content ourselves with looking at it from the other side of the river and then we take the track which goes towards Avanos, for ÇAVUS IN, a village four kilometres away, where we see a long battlement, pierced with little openings, leading to dwellings hollowed out of the rock. The rupestral Church of St. John the Baptist with its interesting architectural decoration has been carved into this rocky wall.

A gate with blind arcades used to be preceded by a colonnade with Ionic Byzantine capitals which have, for the most part, fallen down and which were surmounted by a cornice with modillions. The rectangular doors are surrounded with mouldings after the manner of the Christian sanctuaries of Syria, as in the basilica of St. Simeon Stylites at Qalaat Seman. In the interior the nave is separated from the aisles by heavy arcades, and the rather badly damaged paintings illustrate the life of St. John the Baptist. At the end of the apse a seat with arm rests and a circular bench have been carved out of the rock behind the altar.

To the left of the rocky battlements, we see what looks like an astonishing field of mushrooms. It is in fact cones capped with black rocks, and, a short distance away, to the north, in an imposing tower of rock, stands a most interesting church known as the *Pigeon House of Çavus In*. Thanks to a ladder, provided by the owner to whom one gives a tip, it is possible to go inside. The narthex is in ruins, but we can see the remains of paintings with very well-preserved colours. The frescoes in the nave are extremely beautiful, and may have been the work of Armenians since, to the left of the protheses, is depicted on horseback Mleh, "Melias the Magistrate", the great Armenian leader who fought the Byzantines. In the protheses there are portraits of the Emperor Nicephoros Phocas, the Emperors Theophania, Caesar Bardas and the Curopalate Leon which enable us to date the paintings as 965.

To the south east of Cavus In, at the foot of Ak Tepe (the white hill), there are several parallel valleys scattered with rose-coloured cones. In the second of these, called *Güllü Dere* (valley of roses), we can see, halfway up, a remarkable church with a flat roof ornamented with reliefs of decorative circles, crosses, etc., where a large apse is adorned with paintings of the second half of the 9th century, illustrating the legends of Theophania.

In the third valley, Kizil Ckur (the red valley), we can see, after having gone through two little tunnels, a great cone rising up out of the middle of cultivated fields. An entrance at a first chapel has floral and geometric decorations and may go back to the time of the Iconoclasts; a second chapel, where the frescoes illustrate the childhood of the Virgin, according to a Syrian-Armenian version of the apochryphal version of St. James, are of the end of the 9th century or the beginning of the 10th, which are very rare subjects treated in a most graceful style.

To the north of Ak Tepe and to the east of Çavus In, along the direct route from Ürgüp to Avanos, we can still see the interesting site of ZILVE with its numerous capped cones where some are divided up again like strange bouquets of flowers. We find here anchorite and Stylite cells including the hermitage of the monk Simeon. In the village, a semi-rupestral mosque has a minaret with columns.

We now turn our steps towards GÖREME, the most celebrated site of rupestral Cappadocia, where we find assembled together the most astonishing troglodyte churches, covered with frescoes, of this region.

We see, first of all, at the entrance, one of the best preserved rock churches of Göreme, and also the largest, the *Tokali kilise* (the church of the ring), protected by a grille.

This church, apart from the entrance which has collapsed, is composed of two distinct elements : a very simple vaulted room used as a narthex, out of which opens a huge church. The first is decorated with quite simple paintings in bright colours which run in the form of a frieze, as though it were a picture book illustrating the Life and the Passion of Christ. The message of these paintings is stressed by numerous inscriptions taken from Canonical texts or from the Apocrypha. It is a style of decoration which we meet in many Cappadocian churches of the 9th and 10th centuries. Besides the gospels, the painters were often inspired by an Apocrypha known as the Synoptic Gospel of St. James.

The second church is much more sophisticated in style. The barrel vaults have cross-ribs and the nave terminates, to the east, in a large wide transept added much later and five apses with projecting arches. The walls are decorated with several rows of blind arcades which also have projecting arches and give a strongly Cappadocian aspect, thanks to the red linear decoration.

In contrast, the paintings are certainly the work of artists from an important centre which must have been Constantinople. At this time, in fact, relations were very close between the capital and Cappadocia, a region which had even given

an emperor to the Empire—Nicephoros II Phocas. It was
perhaps in his reign, and certainly during the second half of
the 10th century, that these frescoes were carried out. The
decorative effect is as remarkable for its lifelike quality as for
the richness of the design. Evangelical scenes figure in the dome,
in the frieze around the naos and in the curve of the central
apse which is, besides, an anomaly. The effigies of *St. Michael,
St. George, St. Christopher* carrying his staff which miracu-
lously bursts into leaf, *St. Basil,* etc., fill up all the available
space. Inscriptions are written with very great care and the
scenes which comprise a number of characters, like the *Crucifixion* in the central apse, are just as beautifully arranged as
the simpler compositions such as *Christ Enthroned between two
Archangels* in the second apse to the left.

In spite of the faded colours—only the deep blue of the
background is preserved—we can admire the grace of the design
and the harmonious rhythm of line.

There is now an entrance for the tour of the churches and
we first pass the custodian's house and begin with the group
of churches built on the classical Byzantine plan of an inscribed
cross in a square with a central dome resting on four columns
with pendentives—one, the *Carikli Kilise* has only two but the
apses are projecting as is the usual case in Cappadocia. They
are also preceded by a narthex.

The painted decorations are very similar even though the
range of colours differs from one church to another. The large
panels are devoted to scenes with a number of characters—
scenes from the life of Christ with a liturgical significance—
whilst figures of saints are placed under the arches or on the
piers and the portraits of saints in medallions in the corners or
on the pendentives. Purely ornamental decoration is abundant
and varied but sometimes rather tortured and exaggerated.
Architecturally and decoratively these churches date from the
11th or 12th centuries.

The first one we come to, *Elmali Kilise* (the Church of the

Apple), called thus because of the dwarf apple trees which grow near the entrance, is accessible through a narrow shaft. It is covered with domes on pendentives. Scenes of the life of Christ, from the Nativity to the Resurrection are represented on the vaults, and saints and prophets on the pendentives, also portraits of Christ and archangels in medallions and, in the central apse, a *Deisis* with the *Virgin* and *St. John the Baptist interceding before Christ in Majesty.* In places, where the paint has flaked off, we can see a very simple red linear decoration applied directly to the tufa. This was the usual method when a church was not decorated with frescoes.

We then see the *Barbara Kilise*, a little church where several paintings have themes borrowed from the iconographic repertoire in use after the restoration of images : representations of Christ, of many male and female saints of which *St. Barbara* is one.

We come to the *Yilanli Kilise* (the church of the circus) where, among the figures depicted, are the Emperor Constantine and St. Helena.

The *Karanlik Kilise*, a rather sombre church, is the most interesting of the columned churches because it is part of an important monastery whose rooms we can visit, in particular the refectory with its tables and benches formed out of the rock. The whole ensemble is hollowed into a rocky peak, itself partly collapsed and presenting a noble staging of archature. Beautiful frescoes deal with the *Life of Christ*, and, particularly noteworthy in the narthex, is an *Ascension*, unfortunately defaced by vandals, which is a typical example of the mannered and exaggerated style of the time of the Comnenes. We should also notice in the nave, a *Nativity of Christ* to which has been added the episode of the Magi bringing their offerings, whilst their horses are tied up to a tree and, in the apparition to the shepherds, the charming motif of a little flute player.

The same theme is to be found in the *Çarikli Kilise* (the Church of the Sandal) where two footprints under the Ascension, are claimed to imitate those of Christ at Jerusalem. This is a rather smaller church, but the frescoes are very pleasant in colour. As well as the *Ascension*, they represent the *Nativity*, the *Crucifixion* and the *Four Evangelists*.

After returning to the custodian's house, we can go back to the *Tokali Kilise* which we looked at on arrival, to see several other little sanctuaries carved into the rock. An iron stairway enables us to reach the chapel of St. Eustace of the 10th century ornamented with very well preserved naïve paintings in bright colours. Their style and the errors in the inscriptions would attribute them to the Armenians. The eastern part has been redressed and repainted in the 11th and 12th centuries. We should notice, close to the robe of the angel of the prothesis, graffiti of the 12th century.

We should also notice the tiny little *Chapel of the Theotokos* where the vaulted nave is decorated with paintings of the end of the 9th century or the beginning of the 10th with ghostly silhouettes of figures with great eyes and hooked noses. A cornice with modillions stresses the lines of the vault. Next we come to the chapel of St. Barbe where the red linear decoration is full of variety, the chapels of St. George and St. John the Baptist both covered with frescoes, and, on the side of the road, the impressive mass of *Kizlar Kilise*, the Palace of the Virgin, with numerous communicating rooms including several chapels.

For those who would like to stay longer, I shall indicate easy and interesting excursions to be carried out either from Ürgüp or Üçhisar, but it is preferable, given the bad state of the roads, and sometimes the difficulty of finding the way, to hire a car with an experienced chauffeur.

First of all, I will indicate the churches to be found in the different valleys around Göreme.

At the height of the rocky screen which separates the valley of Göreme from the valley of El Nazar we see the recently discovered rock church aptly called *Sakli Kilise* (the Hidden Church). The paintings which date from the beginning of the

13th century are in an exceptional state of preservation.

The plan is of a transversal nave with three apses and the exceptionally gifted and original painter combines the influence of Constantinople with local popular tradition. This is characterized by the grace of the attitudes, the confident design and the monumental grandeur of composition.

In the valley of El Nazar (the View) one does, in fact have a superb panorama. A little further to the north, a church, constructed in a cone, has some graceful paintings with a predominence of sea green, a favourite colour with Cappadocian painters.

In the valley of Kilicar (the Sword), so named because of the blade-like cones, to the east of Göreme, we find a church in the form of a Greek cross which is the first of this kind in the region. It is decorated with beautiful, predominantly pink paintings.

Other churches are scattered in two valleys to the south of Ürgüp and Üçhisar.

The *Church of St. Theodore* in the valley of Susam Bavri has a flat-roofed nave followed by a projecting apse with a funerary chapel on the right. Besides figures of saints and angels, it is decorated with an archaic series of the Annunciation to the Ascension which is the richest of Cappadocia. In the apse, a *Christ in Majesty* is surrounded by the animals of the Apocalypse. Traces of repainting can be seen and some decorations in relief.

Further to the west, at Kipiz (*Sarrica Kilise*) a yellowish church is carved out of an ochre cone isolated in a small amphitheatre in the middle of fields. It was once part of a monastery which was built into peaks and walls of rock in the surroundings. This church has a most original plan—that of an inscribed cross combined with a triple dome. All the western part has collapsed and the original floor is covered with more than a metre of rubble. The paintings, which have deteriorated and turned black, are characteristic of the middle of the 11th century. They represent scenes from the life of the Virgin and of Christ, and in the apse is a Deisis in gloomy colours.

In the direction of Babayan, now called Ibrahimpaşa, to the left of the road and isolated, is *Tavşan Kilise* (the Church of the Hares)—a name which seems to be due to a mistaken interpretation of the kids painted in the church. We can read the inscription, dated 913–919, which is the oldest in Cappadocia, naming Constantine VI Porphyrogenetus. The frescoes in the church date from this period.

At about 2 kilometres to the south, the place called Elavra, in a group of rupestral chapels, Haghios Vasilios has an interesting decoration of the time of the Iconoclasts, decorated crosses, floral and geometric motifs. Two figures, of which one might be St. Basil, appear to be of a later date. We can also, by means of hiring a taxi with an experienced chauffeur, get to the valley of Cemil. We leave Ürgüp by the road to Sinasos 3 kilometres further on; not far from our road, and near to the river there are, in the church of the Holy Apostles, some much blackened paintings in the archaic style which form a detailed series of the Life of Christ. They date from the end of the 10th century.

About 5 kilometres further on Sinasos, now called Mustafapaşa, is an ancient Greek village which was flourishing until the beginning of the 19th century. It still has some beautiful old houses, but it is only partially inhabited.

Five kilometres further to the south, we leave, to the right, a place called Gorgoli where there are several insignificant chapels and the remains of a hagiasma dedicated to St. Luke and, just at the beginning of a conical peak, the ancient Sanctuary of the Paneghia. Two kilometres to the south of Cemilköy we shall find, among a group of cones bordering the road surrounded by walnuts and poplars, a place of pilgrimage, very popular with the Greeks until they were ejected from Turkey. We can visit the Monastery of Archangelos, with its huge church and blackened paintings of various periods, its vast refectory with a double table and its rooms with, in one of them, a millstone meant to fill up the entrance in case of enemy invasion.

The *Church of Haghios Stephanos*, in a neighbouring cone, has a most interesting decoration of the first half of the 9th century; motifs of a strictly Iconoclastic style are painted on the flat ceiling—geometric or floral with decorated crosses. To the left, we can make out the cross of St. Euphemia with the portraits of the saint in a medallion, some figures executed later than the Iconoclastic period, and a Communion of the Apostles which may perhaps be earlier.

DAMSA the former bishopric of Tavisos now called Taskinpaşaköy was occupied from the 13th century by the Turks, who have left some wonderful monuments there which unfortunately are in a ruined state. To the left of the road, with the splendid background of the bastion of Fodul Dağ, rises up a vast edifice. The walls have lost their facings but the monumental gateway remains and, on the inside, a delicately decorated alcove.

In the village, the mosque and two *türbes* which go back to the days of Taskinpaşa—that is to say, to the 14th century— have been very much destroyed, but one can see curious sculptured gargoyles representing human beings.

Before reaching Suves, on the right, we shall see another series of cones. One of them contains the *Church of the Forty Martyrs*, with frescoes illustrating the history of the martyr St. Sebastion in the left hand corner. These narrative scenes are unique in Cappadocia. They date from the beginning of the 13th century, and an inscription which is now effaced gave the date as 1216–1270 under the Lascarides of Nicaea. Suveş, the former archbishopric of Sobisos, now called Şahinefendi, is a large village surrounded by trees.

The track crosses a plateau at the end of which a kilometre before reaching the village of Mavrican Güzelö, we can see, to the left, a rupestral church preceded by a little vaulted narthex which is as interesting for its architecture—the plan of a cross with a cupola on supports—as for the oriental style of its painting.

The frescoes comprise scenes from the *Life of Christ* with a series of angels under the dome. One is reminded of Coptic or Syrian artists.

In the village, an octagonal building, where the dome is above ground and the rest of it subterranean, is today used as a mosque.

We now ascend the valley from Mavrican to Ortaköy. Halfway up the bank, opposite the village, stands one of the rare churches constructed in the region : St. George, a triple-apsed church of beautiful proportions whose dome has collapsed. Inscriptions in the church in the side chapel give the date of 1293 and the paintings may well be of the 13th century. In the western arm there is a vast *Last Judgement* and, on the drum of the dome, Prophets, seated or crouching, executed in a manner reminiscent of Armenian or Georgian art.

We go the whole length of the river as far as its confluence with the Soğanli which we follow to the little village of the same name. From here, three valleys open out, only to be reached on foot. The first, to the south, Ballik Deresi (the Valley of Fishes) used to have a chapel with paintings in the archaïc style, but it has been transformed into a pigeon house and the paintings have been scratched.

We then follow the Soğanli Dere, but as some of the churches are closed, we must go with the guide from the village who has the keys.

To the left, *Münşil Kilise* has some spoilt paintings which may be the work of the Armenians. At the following tributary, all that remains of the *Ak Kilise* (the White Church) built with a beautiful white facing, have been incorporated into a house. To the left, in a cone which is rather difficult of access, St. Barbe is one of the most interesting churches of the site.

The main nave has kept its paintings dating from 1006 or 1021. They are characterized by the long slender silhouettes, notably the *Seven Sleepers of Ephesus*, in their square frame.

Down below, *Geyik Kilisesi* (the Church of the Stag) owes its name to the animal which accompanied St. Eustace, but the saint has disappeared. The church has two naves and a monolithic iconostasis with a gate and two windows.

Higher up, on the right bank of Soğanli Dere, a group of cones, the *Belli Kilise*, appear where the upper parts are sculptured to form domes. This is the only instance of rock churches with a similar exterior decoration. The churches hollowed out of these cones are in a rather bad state, and two are in use as pigeon houses. The lower chapel of the small cone is a veritable basilica with three aisles separated by pillars. As well as a cycle of the *Life of Christ*, it contains, among the paintings of the 10th and 11th centuries, interesting episodes from *The Lives of the Apostles*.

On the other bank, and almost opposite, a group of cones houses a monastic establishment where the church, the *Karabas Kilise* (the Church of the Black Head), is adorned with very fine paintings of 1060 which overlay a more ancient painting which shows through in certain places. We can discern six portraits of men and women, three of which give the name in the dedication. These portraits have a considerable historic and social significance. In the apse, a *Communion of the Apostles* surmounts a row of *Elders of the Church*. In the vault, there is an Evangelical series.

Finally, 300 metres further on, the church of *Canavar Kilisesi* (the Church of the Monster, because of St. George subduing the dragon) has a double nave. The paintings in the main nave and the apse are effaced, but in the south aisle is a huge *Last Judgement* painted in a funereal style; it is not earlier than the 15th or 16th century. The church was in use until recently.

We come back by the same road, or by Yeşilhisar and, in

this case, we follow the road to Ürgüp which goes through the pretty villages of Basköy, Demirtas and Boyali. We can see, near Tagar, a final rupestral church with a triple apse which is unique for its upper galleries. Its paintings of the 11th to 12th centuries delight us with their bright blue backgrounds, and their decorative motifs.

We now leave the region of Ürgüp to go towards Kayseri and, in order to do so, we must go back to the highway to Nigde.

We go through the village of Incesu and we should note, to the left, an old caravanserai built in 1660 by the grand vizier Kara Mustafa Paşa. Nearby stands a mosque, public baths and a bazaar which together form a vast complex.

KAYSERI is a large city of more than 100,000 inhabitants which is rapidly becoming modernised. It is situated below the foothills of the Erciyan Daği, ancient Mount Argaeus, an extinct volcano, which serves as a background. The old city grew up on the plain between the acropolis hill of ancient *Caesarea* and the medieval fortress. It was at the beginning of the 1st century A.D. that ancient *Eusebeia,* or *Mazaca,* took the name of Caesarea which was then the capital and the principal town of Cappadocia. In the 3rd century, after the defeat of the Roman emperor Valerian at the battle of Edessa, Caesarea was taken by the Sassanid Persians who carried off many captives to Susiana. In the 4th century, a church and a monastery to the north of the town may have been built by St. Basil. It became the centre of the Byzantine complex, then of the Islamic town. During the 6th century the walls were rebuilt on a smaller perimeter.

From the 7th to the 9th century, Caesarea suffered from many Arab invasions and, at the beginning of the second half of the 11th century, a large number of Armenians were driven out of their own country by the Seljuks and settled in the neighbourhood of the town. In 1082 Caesarea was taken by the Seljuks who occupied it until 1243 when the Mongols took

E

over. The Mamelukes were in power in 1419 and the town
was restored to the Ottoman empire in 1515.

We shall begin our visit of Kayseri from the Cumburiyet
Meydani, the Republic Square, a vast esplanade laid out on
the site of an ancient quarter opposite the ramparts of the
citadel.

It is bounded on the north by the Sahibiye Medresesi, a
former school of Koranic theology, now disaffected. The entrance gate, dating from 1267, opens at the back of a deep
recess with the curve decorated with stalactites. The decoration
is extremely delicate and on either side of the arch of the
recess we can see two badly damaged carved heads of lions.

The citadel at the other end of the square has a rampart
whose foundations go back to the time of Justinian. It was
designed by the Seljuk sultan, Kaykavus, at the beginning
of the 13th century towards the year 1224, then restored severel
times, notably in the 16th century in the reign of the Ottoman
sultan, Mohammed II. The fortifications of the town, which
also go back to the time of Justinian, are now almost destroyed.

The *enceinte* of the citadel, constructed of blocks of lava,
is flanked by nineteen square or rectangular towers which used
to command the parapet walk.

Two gates lead to the interior preceded by a barbican. The
one to the south west is a double gate; the second, which
opens round an angle of a 30 metre corridor, is defended by
a projecting tower. We should notice here and there on the
ogival vaulted door a carving of a lion which is of Seljuk
origin. Above the lower door is an inscription of 1465 with
the name of Sultan Mohammed II.

The interior of the fortress now serves as a market place.
Almost opposite the gate, against the inner face of the curtain
wall, is the little mosque, *Fatih Camii*, erected by Sultan
Mohammed II Fatih in the 15th century on the site of an
oratory built by a prince of the Karamanoglu dynasty.

Most of the towers open onto the interior of the citadel,

except for four much larger constructions which comprise several storeys with wooden floors.

Leaving the citadel by the south west gate which communicates with the city, we follow along the walls which in this section still have fragments of the bray which reinforced them and which were preceded by a broad deep moat, now filled in.

We come out into a very big square with three ancient monuments at the far end.

Huant Medrese, a former school of theology, now houses an archaeological museum. It was built in the 13th century a little later than the neighbouring mosque of 1237. It has a superb portal, opening onto the square, with an arch decorated with stalactites.

Through a little entrance hall with an alcove which serves as a porter's lodge, we reach the courtyard, surrounded by porticoes on three sides with, at the end, a large *iwân* which used to open onto a portico which has disappeared.

The rooms and galleries contain antiquities of all periods, more particularly Hittite antiquities and ceramics of Kültepe of the 3rd millennium. We can also see the *türbe* of the Princess Mahperi the founder of the mosque and of the *medresesi*.

The *Honat Hatum Camii* stands at the end of a lane and has a recently reconstructed portal flanked by a minaret. Once through the entrance, we pass beneath a gallery surrounding a little courtyard where stands the *türbe*, the interior of which we have just seen. From the outside it has eight faces richly decorated with inscriptions and interlacings with little columns at the corners.

The prayer hall of the mosque is formed of eight aisles separated by seven rows of pillars.

On leaving the mosque, we see a *türbe* of the time of the Seljuks, then, at the end of a narrow street, stands the *Han Camii* (the caravanserai mosque). We then follow the Cunhuriyet Meydani by car to visit the *Döner Kümbet* (the revolving mausoleum), the most interesting monument of Kayseri, which

is a kilometre away. It was cleared from the houses which
surrounded it a few years ago. It is a cylindrical tower standing on a high square base with mitred corners surmounted by
a cylindro-conical roof. The decoration is very fine; in particular the arabesques and palm leaves which adorn the blind
arches surrounding the building.

The entrance doorway which leads to a room in the tower
is surmounted by two bas-reliefs representing feline forms with
human heads. The inscription above the door states that the
mausoleum was built by Sah Cihan Hatun in about 1275.

A little further on but to the left, the *Sirçali Kümbet*, or
Faience Tower, is a mausoleum also built on a square base
above which there is a twelve-sided room originally covered
by a pyramid roof which has disappeared. Likewise the decoration of glazed tiles which may have faced certain parts of the
türbe of the middle of the 14th century have disappeared.

We return to the main square and continue into the bazaar
quarter. Near the *Bedestan* we reach the *Ulu Camii*, the Great
Mosque, dominated by a tall minaret.

Built during the first half of the 13th century under the
Danismendides, but modernized, it comprises a large prayer hall
with five aisles separated by four rows of pillars of which some
are of antique origin. The cylindrical minaret, built of brick
upon a square base and an octagonal drum, has a balcony
with an encorbelment of stalactites. The section above the
balcony is of the Ottoman period.

Opposite, the *Vizir Han*, the Caravanserai of the Viziers,
is a huge structure of no particular interest built of blocks of
grey lava like most of the old houses of Kayseri.

Continuing along the narrow street which follows the *Ulu
Camii* we shall come to the *Hatuniye Medresesi* after having
passed the *Melik Gazi Medresesi*, former School of Theology.

This *medrese*, built in 1431 by Melik en Nasir Mohammed,
is entered through a portal with a pointed arch flanked by two
niches. We then enter a courtyard surrounded by porticoes.

Opposite is an *iwan* covered by a barrel vault ending in a cloister vault flanked by two rooms with domes resting on a frieze of triangles with twelve facets. Amongst the columns which support the porticoes are some Ionic and Corinthian capitals taken from buildings of antiquity.

Nearby stands *Hatiroğlu Camii*, a little mosque of only slight interest, close to the encircling wall which used to protect the city. It is not far from the *Lala Paşa Camii*, a small 14th-century mosque which we can also pass by.

In contrast we can see near the Dukkan Onü Square the *Güllück Camii*, one of the oldest mosques of the town, built in 1210. The prayer hall has five aisles and is covered with pointed barrel vaults and two domes resting on pillars.

If we return near the Republic square, we shall find the *Kurşunlu Camii* built in 1584 which is entered through a portico with five bays. The hall of the *mirhab* is square in plan and covered with a dome supported by four pendentives. Above the door an inscription in gold on a green background mentions the name of the founder, Ahmet Paşa. It may possibly be the work of the famous architect Sinan, since it is in keeping with his design and inspiration.

Finally let us notice the *Çifte Medrese* (the double Medrese), a complex of buildings in a very ruinous condition erected in 1205 comprising a *medrese* and a hospital, and the oldest building of this type. It includes, over and above the normal plan of a *medrese*, examination halls and rooms for the administration of the hospital.

We now have the choice of either continuing to Sivas where we come to Itinerary III or to go on to Ankara.

I will describe the itinerary to Sivas. After 4 kilometres we shall see on the right of the road the Çifte Kumbet.

Eight kilometres further on, a causeway cut into the rock still subsists for 100 metres. It must have been the work of the Hittites.

At the 19th kilometre, on reaching two petrol pumps we

turn off to the left along a track which crosses the railway and after 2 kilometres takes us to the ancient Kanesh, the ruins of which lie beneath a large tumulus, known as KÜLTEPE, to the left of the track. A second tumulus to the right marks the site of the Assyrian commercial quarter.

The origins of Kültepe go back to the third millenium, before the great migration of the Indo-europeans. During the first half of the 24th century B.C., the city must have been under the rule of Sargon, king of Akkab in Mesopotamia. A Hittite text, inscribed several centuries later, records a coalition of 17 kings against a successor of Sargon, Naram Sin (c. 2320–2284 B.C.) among whom there was a certain Zipani, king of Kanesh.

Before the arrival of the Hittites, a type of pottery called Cappadocian, decorated with symbols and geometric designs was made at Kanesh. This kind of ceramic, which existed alongside other more ancient styles, usually monochrome, gradually disappeared on the arrival of the Hittites who brought a different kind of ceramic with them, also monochrome, but with more varied and refined shapes like the jug with a lip in the museum at Ankara. The Hittite city was founded on the site of Boğazköy at a time when Cappadocian pottery was beginning to disappear.

Towards the 19th century B.C. there was an important colony of Assyrian merchants at the gates of the town outside the encircling wall. Caravans took merchandise as far as Mesopotamia and even to the Indus Valley and the Mediterranean. Tablets written in Assyrian and found on the site of their *karum* give valuable information concerning this period. After having prospered for two or three centuries, this *karum* must have been burnt down during a war between rival Hittite princes.

The Hittite city was itself destroyed towards 1200 by the Phrygians who laid out a town on its ruins. Kanesh gradually declined and was only an insignificant town in the Hellenistic period.

After arriving at the foot of the tumulus, we take a path to the left and climb up the side. The very size of the tumulus indicates what a large city Kanesh was in Hittite times. Among those ruins which are still visible we will notice several sections of walls of brick partly vitrified after a fire, with here and there fragments of pottery or large half-buried pitchers.

On the mound of the city where the king of Kanesh lived, the remains of a palace have been excavated. It is contemporary with the second Assyrian warehouse, about 19th century B.C., which was burnt down at the same time. Some of the royal correspondence and a list of palace officials have been found. The buildings which have been unearthed, differ architecturally from the Assyrian *karum*. A large temple has also been found. Then, on the site of the palace, several edifices of the megaron type were erected under the new Hittite empire in its turn ravaged towards 1200 B.C.

Excavations have also brought to light the ramparts of the town of the Phrygian period. They are six metres thick and built on Hittite foundations.

Seven kilometres further on, we leave to the right the road to Malatya by which we could reach KARAY HAN 15 kilometres away, a Seljuk caravanserai completed in about 1240. It lies a kilometre from the highway, in the village of Bünyan where there is also a picturesque waterfall.

We should notice particularly the variety of shapes of the bastions which go round the periphery of the building and, after having passed through the portal, we cross an *iwân* to reach the court surrounded by vaulted loggias and, opposite, stands the Great Hall. This comprises a single nave with seven bays of which one has a dome. It was erected between the year 1230 and 1236. In a corner of the courtyard a mosque is covered with a dome; the niche of the *mirhab*, decorated with stalactities is in a bad state of preservation.

We now return to the road to Sivas and see further on to the left, the Tüz Gölu (the Salt Lake), the ancient Palas Lake near which is to be found the little town of Aipolioi, seat of a bishopric in Byzantine times.

Then we see on the right, one of the most interesting caravanserais of the whole of Anatolia, the SULTANHANI, situated in the village of the same name. It was built during the Seljuk period between 1232 and 1236.

The portal, which has just been restored, was surmounted with a stalactite arch with on each side of the door a cluster of five little oval columns. Each of the two corners of the façade are reinforced with a buttress in the form of an hexagonal star with one of the points inserted into the façade. We then come into a rectangular courtyard flanked by two columned galleries. In the centre of the courtyard and in the axis of the building stands a strange little oratory supported by four pillars linked by pointed arches handsomely moulded and decorated with serrations and a braid carved into the stone of a lovely ochre patina. A little door reached up a narrow and steep spiral staircase leads to a prayer hall with a *mirhab*.

The left hand gallery is supported by a double colonnade forming seven bays with pointed barrel vaults. The right hand gallery has also seven bays but the vaults are only supported by a single row of columns and upon a wall which separates the gallery of rooms used as shops. There is a *hammam* with four rooms in the west corner of the courtyard.

The back of the caravanserai is composed of a high central nave with a pointed barrel-vault flanked by quincunxes of columns which create on each side, seven little transversal aisles above which have been constructed two terraces separated by the arch of the central nave. A lantern on top of a dome rising from a drum supported by four pendentives in the middle of the central aisle is the only form of lighting for this immense hall.

Finally the outer buttresses are furnished with turrets in a variety of shapes.

We then leave the large village of Gemerek to the left and

continue through Şarkişla and go over the Pass of Yasibel, 1,578 metres in altitude, then over Saylar, 1,500 metres which are merely undulations on a plateau which we cross in a straight line.

The road descends towards the Plain of Sivas with its extensive view and we skirt the Kisil Irmac by the Kesik Köprü (the divided bridge) formed by two bridges linked by an embankment.

We then come to Sivas which is described in Itinerary III.

Anyone wishing to go direct to Ankara must leave Kayseri by the Istanbul Caddesi and, leaving to the right the road to Sivas then on the left the road to Nigde, continue towards Kirsehir. This road has nothing of interest until we reach the little town of Kirsehir situated a short distance from the road to the left.

KIRSEHIR may be the ancient Justinianopolis-Mokyssos which Justinian raised to the level of a city in about A.D. 536. From the 14th to the 18th centuries it was the centre of a powerful religious sect called the Ahis. The founder of the monastery of Ahiören at Kirsehir was formerly a tanner and the first initiates of the sect were often craftsmen of this powerful fraternity. They travelled to Asia Minor to extend their sphere of influence and often succeeded in settling the differences between the Anatolian princes to their own advantage.

Eskişehir is a lively little modernized town, which has developed since the time when several industries were established. The *Kurşunlu Camii*, built in 1525 in the reign of Süleyman the Magnificent, may be the work of Sinan.

The *Alâeddin Camii* was founded in 1262 by Giyaseddin Keyhüsrey III, a Seljuk sultan. He was also responsible for several *türbes*. The finest of all is to be found on the Ankara road to the right. It is entered through a very handsome porch with a high pointed barrel vault protecting a sort of shell. The decoration is graceful and restrained.

A hundred kilometres further on we skirt the Kizil Irmak
over a very much restored old ass-backed bridge of the Seljuk
period. As we approach Ankara we follow the lake of Gölbasi.
We are now in the outskirts of Ankara and soon arrive in the
centre.

ANKARA is above all a modern town with wide boulevards,
imposing administrative offices and noisy traffic. But we must
not forget that its origins are very ancient and that over and
above its archaeological museum which needs to be visited
with care there are old quarters and monuments which are
not without interest.

Let us see what is left of the ancient town. First there are
the Roman Baths discovered by chance in 1926 near the
Çankiri Caddesi. They date from the beginning of the 3rd
century A.D. and they were composed of a dozen great rooms
among which we can distinguish the *caldarium*, the *tepidarium*,
and the *frigidarium*. We notice here and there drains, remains
of marble flooring and fragments of statues. In each case it is
the basements which are the best preserved with their little
columns faced in brick which used to support the floors of
different rooms.

The *palaestra*, less well-preserved than the Baths, was rectangular in plan and surrounded by a broad portico. It was
probably built in the 2nd century A.D. as well as the bathing
pool with which it communicates.

We shall then find on the Hükûmet Meydani, in the centre
of a little garden, a Roman column called the column of
Julian. It was probably erected in honour of this emperor
after his sojourn in Ankara in 362.

Not far from here lies the most interesting Roman building
of ancient Ankara, the imposing remains of the Temple of
Augustus and of Rome of the 2nd century A.D. which may have
been restored and rearranged in the time of Augustus. It was
probably turned into a church at the beginning of the 6th
century and then later replaced by a little Turkish mosque.

In its final state the temple was surrounded by a portico of which the bases of the columns and some Corinthian capitals still subsist. It was supported on a substructure reached by seven steps. The entrance to the *cella* and the two *antae* is in a good state of preservation. On the left *anta* some Latin verses have been inscribed to the honour of Augustus.

To the left of the temple, the little *Mosque of Haci Bayram* was founded at the beginning of the 15th century by Haci Bayram whose *türbe* we see nearby.

We now climb up to the temple which comprises two *enceintes* both built in the Byzantine period; the first, which crowns the summit of the rocky peak dominating the town, was erected there towards 620 by Heraclius after the defeat of the Sassanid king Khosrow Parviz, or during the reign of Constantine II when Arab invasions were frequent. Moreover it was taken several times, notably in 695, then in 708 by the Calif of Walid. It was then in vain restored by Leon II, the Isaurian, since the Arabs besieged it in 797. Nicephorus I restored the town once more and again it was able to resist the troops of Haroun el Rachid. The breaches were repaired and Michael II, the Stammerer, then built the second wall, but this did not prevent the Pauliciens from seizing it in 871 and they held it until 931 at which time it fell into the hands of the Arabs.

The first *enceinte* which is 1,500 metres long comprised 14 square bastions and four semi-cylindrical towers flanked by two gates. Only twelve of the square towers and three of the semi-cylindrical towers remain. This first wall is built of quite regular rows of blocks of stone, for the most part taken from the ancient monuments of the lower town, whilst the merlons of the parapet are in brick.

After skirting the west side of the fortress, we pass in front of a building with little domes, the *bedestan* constructed in the second half of the 15th century in the reign of Mohammed II Fatih. It houses the Hittite museum. Here there are, not only statues, figurines, pottery and jewels of every period, but also splendid sculpture and complete Hittite monuments.

We then come to the principal gateway of the lower *enceinte* called Hisar Kapisi. It is flanked by two bastions with rounded tops. A second wall with a bay in the axis of the preceding entrance was raised between two towers, thus forming a little interior courtyard. The arch, made of two coloured stone and serving as a lintel, is an addition by the Ottomans.

We then continue straight through an old quarter and after 200 metres we reach the second *enceinte* near the Parmak Kapisi the most remarkable work of the whole citadel.

The upper citadel which is 1,150 metres long is flanked by pentagonal bastions set very close to each other to the south where they are almost rectangular. The walls are built of great blocks of stone taken from the ancient monuments of the town. Thus, in the curtain wall which links the two bastions flanking the Parmak Kapisi, we notice several reclining statues of Priapus and a number of altars. The upper part of the walls which are sometimes more than 6 metres high, is constructed of alternate rows of brick and stone.

The Finger Gate or *Parmak Kapisi* is formed of a rectangular bastion pierced with two staggered bays. The outer gate opens to the right so that the assailant cannot obtain protection from it.

To the right of the gate, a strong polygonal tower, oval on the inside, the *Şark Kale*, supports both the first and the second wall. Constructed after the erection of the first citadel, it was reinforced in the reign of Michael II, the Stammerer. The thickness of the walls was then increased to five or six metres. The rows of stone of this reinforcement overlaps those of the second wall.

After having passed through the double gate, we leave, to the right the *Mosque of Ala et Tin* which has a fine *mimber* of the 12th century and cross the upper town to reach *Ak Kale*, the White Fortress, erected in the Ottoman period on the foundations of a Byzantine wall. These dominate the Gorge of Bent Deresi at the end of which is a dam linked to the fortress by a series of outworks, mostly constructed under the first Ottomans.

In the old town, which has several quarters with narrow tortuous streets, are some mosques, but they are of limited interest. It is worth noting that *Ahi Elvan Camii*, rectangular in plan and built towards the end of the 14th century, has a delightful *mimber* and capitals taken from Byzantine and Roman monuments.

Not far from here, the *Arslanhane Camii*, the Mosque of the Menagerie, attributed to the Emir Seyf et Tin at the beginning of the 13th century is the oldest and largest of Ankara. It takes its name from a stone lion of the Roman period which can be seen in the courtyard. It comprises several antique fragments incorporated into the base of the minaret, and capitals and bases of Roman and Byzantine columns in the prayer hall where the roof is supported by 24 wooden columns. The *mirhab* is in mosaic of glazed faience and the upper part has stalactite decorations. To the right, a *mimber* of carved walnut is dated 1290. The *türbe*, in which the remains of the founder lie, was built on the foundations of a Roman building. In the neighbouring houses there are also a number of fragments from antiquity.

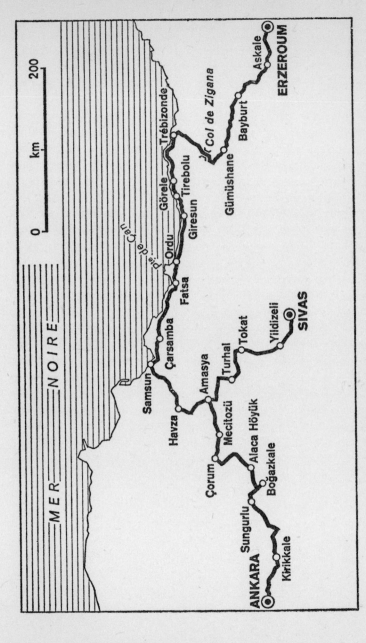

FROM ANKARA TO SIVAS, TREBIZOND AND ERZEROUM

ITINERARY III

FROM ANKARA TO SIVAS, TREBIZOND AND ERZURUM

Boğazkale — Yazilikaya — Büyükkale — Alaca
Höyük — Çorum — Amasya — Tokat — Sivas
—Samsun — Ordu — Giresun — Trebizond —
Sumela — Erzurum

ON this itinerary it is possible to link up with Itinerary II at Sivas and to begin the tour of Eastern Turkey with Trebizond and Erzurum. Then we can visit the most interesting of the Hittite sites at Boğazkale, begin a tour of the Armenian churches and explore the regions bordering the Black Sea.

We leave Ankara by an excellent, surfaced road which crosses a fertile plain after 33 kilometres, leaving on one side a road for HASANOGLU, a little village four kilometres away, close to which there are some rather scant rock bas-reliefs which date from the 1st century A.D., the time of the realm of the Tectosages Galatians founded in the 3rd century B.C. by Gallic tribes.

We then come to a mountainous region, leaving the town of Kirikkale to the right, which is of no interest; then, the road to Sivas by Yozgat, and take the one which leads to Samsun and Amasya.

At Sungurlu we take to the right a road which will bring us to the Hittite sites of Boğazkale and Alaca Höyük, a road which is negotiable but unsurfaced.

After 16 kilometres we leave to the left the road which we shall take later on for Alaca Höyük and, at the entrance to the village of BOĞAZKALE, beyond the little local museum, we take the path to the right which leads to the entry to the rock sanctuary of YAZILIKAYA with its famous bas-reliefs. It is laid out in a circle of rocks. The bas-reliefs, cut into the rock face, are dedicated to male and female divinities. The worship of these gods was celebrated in the open air behind a temple whose foundations have been brought to light. On the northern side a corridor room was intended for the Royal cult with the statue of the great king Toudhalija (*c.* 1250–1220 b.c.) which includes the god Sarrouma, the god of the sword, and a theory of twelve divinities. These reliefs, as well as those of the Mountain of the Royal Scrolls are orientated towards the statue to the north.

The king is on a reduced scale compared with the young god. The second relief shows the shaft of a sword with the hilt formed by two reclining lions surmounted by two half-figures of lions and terminating in a human head wearing the divine tiara.

The bas-reliefs of the principal sanctuary frame a panel representing the mystical marriage of the god Teshub who holds a mace in his right hand and a divine emblem in the other, with the goddess Hepatu supported by her animal emblem, the lion. She is wearing a cylindrical tiara and holds out an emblem to Teshub whilst the god is supported by two figures personifying the mountains, Nanni and Hazzi. Two animals, probably bulls, represent day and night. Behind the goddess, a young god, Sarrouma her son, rests on an animal and precedes the goddess Mezulla, daughter of the goddess of the sun, Arinna, and the goddess Zinouki, grand-daughter of the goddess Arinna.

This panel, together with those which border it, appears to have been executed during the reign of Hattusili III (*c.* 1275–1250 b.c.). Behind Teshub stands a god who holds a mace and a sword and, another god, the god of agriculture, Telepinu, placed on a mound, personifies mountains. Following him on other rock faces, is a procession of secondary gods, among whom two are winged, the second being the moon god. Behind this latter, surmounted by a winged discus, comes the Hittite god of the sun, the preceding ones being of Hurrite origin. Further on, two genii, bearing a crescent moon, are followed by a cortege of warriors.

On the right of the central panel we see a procession of secondary goddesses who may represent the principal cities of the Hittite empire and a character, holding a divine ideogram in one hand and a baton in the other, who may represent the deified king.

The Hittite sculptors worked according to very precise rules. The features, the hair, the draperies are always represented in the same manner. The arm nearest the spectator is bent and pressed against the body whilst the other is slightly forward. In contrast, the women hold their arms out in front of them, slightly bent in a gesture of offering.

We now return to the village of Boğazkale and, a kilometre further on, we arrive at the ruins of the lower town of ancient *HATTUSA*. The excavations, undertaken in 1906 and continued at later dates, testify that there were five principle periods in the occupation of the site. The first, beginning towards the middle of the 3rd millennium and ending towards the end of the same millennium, during the arrival of the Hittite people.

Hatti, the future *Hattusa*, was occupied towards the end of the 19th century B.C. by Anitta. Labarna II who made it the capital of this empire, took the surname of Hattusa I. The ancient Hittite empire reached its zenith under his rule and under that of his successor, Mursili, who undertook to march upon Babylon which he seized towards 1594 B.C. thus overthrowing the 1st Babylonian dynasty. On his return, he was assassinated by his brother-in-law who seized power. Despite

F

a change of dynasty towards 1460 B.C. the New Hittite Empire continued to be a prey to invasion by its neighbours. Hattusa, the capital, was itself reduced to ashes, but Suppiluliuma, (c. 1375-1335 B.C.) repelled the invaders and took up the policy of Hittite expansion towards Syria. In about the year 1200 B.C., the New Hittite Empire succumbed to the attacks of tribes who had come to Europe via the Bosphorus. These invasions, which Egyptian texts mention under the name of Peoples of the Sea, were so sudden that the Royal archives of Boğasköy do not even mention them. During the two last periods, the occupation of the site was restricted and it was towards the year 1000 B.C. that the complex of buildings situated to the north of the town was restored.

Beyond the remains of a tower which reinforced the ramparts of the lower town, we see, also to the right, the ruins of a temple dedicated to the Hittite god of storms. The foundations subsist on a high terrace with three steps with at its foot either an esplanade or public building separated from the residential quarter by walls.

To the north, were the houses of the Syrian merchants. They comprised a certain number of apartments around a central tower and each house was surrounded by paved pathways.

The remains of a town gate with three openings have also been brought to light and, opposite the temple, a sanctuary of the Phrygian period with a single room which contained an altar made of re-used Hittite blocks and a sacrificial basin.

A little further on, to the left of the road, vestiges of the last phase of the period of the Assyrian colony have been discovered and, more particularly, a house which contains the debris of 56 great pitchers which were partly buried in the earth.

We then continue to follow the path, and, a kilometre further on, we see, to the left, on a height called BÜYÜK-KALE, the ruins of ancient dwelling places of the Hittite kings with their libraries where a number of tablets, shops and a temple etc., have been unearthed.

We first see the building consecrated to the archives. It formed a complex with a building of the 14th or 15th century B.C. It is also in this section of the site that we can best see the defensive system which used to surround the palace. Five ramparts succeed each other; the oldest, built at the time of the Assyrian colony, used to rise up on a base of masonry joined with mortar, surmounted by rectangular sunbaked bricks supported by wooden props and reinforced by rectangular towers.

The second, which constitutes an example of a wall with casemates probably set up in the reign of Hantili in the 16th century B.C., must have measured about nine metres thick. It was really composed of two screens connected by walls of cornerstones forming casemates. It was built on traces of the first wall.

The third, which goes back either to the 14th or 13th century B.C., also comprises interior casemates but is flanked by strong towers constructed of sunbaked bricks on a foundation of stone which already reached seven metres in height in one of the works. A kind of slope of beaten earth used to protect the base of the rampart. Later this beaten earth was covered with paving stones. To this third period belongs the bastion of the south west angle linked to the fortress by a ramp or a stairway from which it was possible to reach the battlement walk of the curtain wall, while access to the area of the palace was reached by a ramp paved with red flagstones which continued to the upper plateau where the courtyards are surrounded by porticoes.

The fourth rampart was raised up on the remains of a wall of the 1st Hittite Empire, after the destruction of Hattusa, whilst the 5th, of the Hellenistic era or even of the Roman, was pierced in this sector with a postern gate set up on the site of a Phrygian gate which has been unearthed.

Buildings which have also been unearthed on the upper terrace had been reconstructed at the end of the New Hittite Empire, at some time after 1280 B.C.

A little further on, the rock of Nisantas bears an inscription in Hittite characters giving the genealogy of Suppilulium I, contemporary of Pharoah Amenophis IV and of the king Nimqad of Ugarit.

We continue to climb in the direction of the summit of the hill and, a kilometre further on, we reached the east front of the *enceinte* of the upper town, near a gate—the Royal gate—vaulted with blocks arranged in encorbelment, but the key block of the vault is missing. It was decorated in relief with the figure of the god Teshub which has been taken to the museum at Ankara. The principle gates were formed of a strong bastion connecting the inner and outer walls. An outer ramp, bent at a right angle, gave access to the entrance gate, abutting at the back of a recess formed by the projections of two great flanking towers. At the back of the recess, a first door leads to an entrance hall constructed in the bastion which communicated with the interior by means of a second door. The gates were constructed of great rectangular blocks, slightly curved, which form ogival apertures. From the casemates of the bastion, loopholes made it possible to annihilate any assailant who set foot in the hall.

Following the rampart on the inner side, we find successive remains of three temples; the *cella* was preceded by two chambers whose entrances were arranged in such a manner that it was not possible to see the statue of the god from the courtyard. Only the priest and high dignitaries had access to the *cella*. The clergy were given charge of caring for the God, looking to his subsistance and carrying out the ceremonial anointments due to him. Before being allowed to officiate, the priest had to be in a state of ritual purity. As well as this, they had to be responsible for guarding the temple during the night, and any one of them who might have passed the night in the city with his wife was put to death. In the course of the sacrificial rituals, oxen, sheep, goats and, more rarely, dogs and pigs were killed.

Among the festivals celebrated in the temple, one of them consisted of a play illustrating the myth of the slaying by a divine hero of the dragon Illuyankas who personified the spirit of evil. Also enacted was the legend of Telepinu, god of vegetation, similar to the legend of Adonis which used to be presented at the same time at Byblos.

If we continue to climb for another kilometre, we shall arrive at the entrance of a long subterranean passage called Yerkapi which terminated in a postern opening out at the foot of the wall. It is very well-preserved with its safety device of corbels.

Finally, near the end of a path, we can see the famous Gate of the Lion, one of the best preserved monuments of Boğazkale. It is formed of a postern framed by two enormous lions, of which only the foreparts are free of the mass of stone-work.

We should then return to the fork in the road which we pointed out at the beginning, and continue straight on for 13 kilometres. Then, leaving in front of us the road which leads to the village of Alaca, we take, to the left, the one to Alaca Höyük, and it is at the entrance of the hamlet that we see, to the left, the excavation site and the beautiful Gate of the Sphinx, one of the entrances to the ancient Hittite city. It is concerned with Kussara, mentioned in several Hittite texts, whose evolution is explained to us by the different kinds of pottery which have been discovered and collected together in the little museum set up in the centre of the village.

A strong rampart built of great blocks of stone defended the city in the time of the Hittites. It was pierced with several gates of which the most important, the Gate of the Sphinx, still has the two sphinxes who forbade evildoers access to the city. On one of the door jambs a bas-relief represents a Hittite dog reclining on a double-headed eagle holding a rabbit in his claws. The two flanking towers which defended access to the gate no longer exist.

We then see the remains of a temple of the New Hittite Empire.

To return to the highway, we continue in the same direction.

ÇORUM which we soon reach, is an industrial town where there is nothing of interest except the *Ulu Camii*, the Great Mosque founded in the 13th century during the Seljuk period and restored in the 19th century.

We continue to follow the road to Samsun which goes through Mecitözü, a large village situated near the site of ancient *Etonea* and not far from which we can see, at Isiklar, several rock tombs.

Fifty kilometres further on we take the road to the right which leads to Amasya and Sivas.

AMASYA is a delightful place situated in a gorge of Yesil Irmak, whilst to the south of the town there stretches an amphitheatre of hills. From the other side of the river it is dominated by a high screen of rock on which are built the walls of a fortress and the entrances to rock tombs.

The fortress which commands the gorge is earlier than the conquest of Asia Minor by Alexander the Great. During the Hellenistic period Ancient *Amaseia* became the capital of the kings of Pontis, then the principle city of a Roman province. The geographer, Strabo, was born there. During the Byzantine period, the fortress of *Amaseia* was part of the deme of Armeniakon. Taken in 712 by the Caliph Walid I, it was recaptured a little later by the Byzantines. Profiting from the fratricidal wars in which the Byzantines were engaged, the Turks seized the city which in the 13th century was stormed by the Mongols but resisted the assaults of Tamerlaine. Nicknamed the Bagdad of Roum in the Middle Ages, it remained in the possession of the Ottoman sultans who repeatedly made it their seat of government. The city declined in the 19th century and became a little provincial town with no comparison with the city when it was under the rule of Rome or during the Middle Ages.

Whilst the modern town and different Moslem buildings succeed each other up the north bank, the rocky cliff which rises up on the south bank is riddled with the ruins of different fortresses which succeeded each other for the defence of this ford which was of strategic importance. At the time of Strabo two walls from the upper citadel descended the rock right to the river and they were linked along the banks by a wall which used to enclose the ancient town. In the Middle Ages the suburb established on the right bank of Yesil Irmak was more important than the town on the left bank.

Of the citadel itself there only remain sections of curtain wall and of towers of different periods intermingled with tombs of the Hellenistic era, in one of which some French soldiers were incarcerated during the Egyptian war in 1801.

On the right bank, we shall see successively : the *Torumtay Türbesi* built in 1266 by Torumtay. It is quite graceful with its stalactite windows and outside staircase. Opposite stands the *Gök Medrese Camii*, the mosque of the Blue Medrese, erected in 1276 and now disaffected and transformed into a museum. The portal, opening in the northern façade where the corners are reinforced by cylindrical buttresses on square bases, is preceded by several steps and flanked by two windows with arches decorated with stalactities. To the left, and recessed into the façade, stands a very graceful *türbe* which we can reach by means of a staircase constructed against the transverse wall of the mosque. It is lighted by three windows in tiercepoint and the funerary chamber is covered with a pyramid supported by an octagonal drum ornamented with glazed bricks.

The prayer hall has three aisles, each of which is covered by five cupolas resting on two rows of four cruciform pillars. The plan and the architecture bring to mind Byzantine basilicas with a central aisle broader than the side aisles.

On the other side of the road, the *Yörgüç Paşa Camii* built in 1428 by Yörgüç Paşa, one of the viziers of Sultan

Mohammed I, is a charming little mosque preceded by a large porch with a dome. The flanking room to the right contains three tombs including one of the founder. The complex of buildings standing to the north, a hostel and a *medrese*, is also attributed to this vizier.

The quarter crossed by the main road is composed of old and picturesque houses in the centre of which there are several *türbes*. To the left, the *Şehzadeler Türbesi*, a little farther on, the *Şehzade Türbesi*, then to the right along a narrow parallel street, the *Halifet Gazi Türbesi*, the *Şadgeldi Türbesi*, and the *Sultan Mesut Türbesi*.

The first one to the left, the *Şehzadeler Türbesi*, built in 1410 by Sultan Mahommed I, contains the tombs of several princes of the Imperial family; the *Şehzade Türbesi*, covered with a dome supported on pillars linked by arches, may have contained the tomb of a son of Sultan Beyazit I. The *Halifet Gazi Türbesi*, erected by a vizier of the Emir Damismendide Melik Gazi towards 1145, has an octagonal funerary chamber on a high square sub-structure which contains the grave vault. It is covered by a dome surmounted by a pyramid with eight faces. The *medrese* which used to stand nearby is now in ruins.

The last mausoleum, the *Sultan Mesut Türbesi*, which dates from the 15th century, is formed of a vault constructed in a basement over which the funerary chamber is built.

We soon reach the imposing *Sultan Beyazit Camii*, a mosque in the Ottoman style, built in 1486 by the Sultan Beyazit II. It is preceded by a large terrace shaded by plane trees and bordered by an avenue which follows the bank of the river. On the terrace is an ablutions fountain and a second fountain.

The portico, with five arches covered by cupolas resting on antique columns with stalactite capitals, is framed by two minarets with a single balcony supported on projecting foundations. The entrance gate, with stalactites in the middle of the portico, is flanked by two prayer niches. Here the faithful, who arrived late, could pay their devotions without disturbing the congregation.

The hall of the *mihrab* has two bays, each covered with a dome resting on four pendentives. Besides the *mihrab* and the *mimber*, which are of marble, we should notice the facing of glazed tiles covered with inscriptions in white on a blue ground which decorate the tympanums of the windows.

Near the mosque a *medrese* built by Beyazit II comprises three blocks of buildings surrounded by porticoes with, to the south, a prayer hall covered with a dome.

From there we can cross the wooden bridge which takes us to the other bank and the quarter enclosed between the hills and the river. We see, on the left, two tombs of the Hellenistic era cut out of the rock, a little mosque, and an oratory founded by one of the women of Sultan Beyazit, whilst, opposite, a supporting wall flanks the terrace on which stood the palace of the former kings of Pontis, restored by the Seljuks and the Ottomans.

Above the terrace, three tombs cut out of the rock date from the Hellenistic period; the one on the left was transformed into a chapel in the Byzantine era, and nearby emerge three tunnels hollowed into the rock. All sorts of hypotheses have been made as to the origin of these tunnels which perhaps served to supply the garrison with water or to facilitate the movement of troops.

We now go back to the other bank where we can see the *Kileri Süleyman Ağa Camii*, founded in 1485 by Kileri Selim Ağa with, behind it and very much in ruins, the *Tag Hani*, a caravanserai dating from 1698, and the *Burmari Minare Camii*, the mosque with a minaret in cable form built in the reign of Sultan Kaihorsrow II towards 1245. Like the *Gök Medrese* or the great mosque of Divrigi, this is a Seljuk edifice which, on account of its elongated shape and central aisle larger than the side aisles, skilfully vaulted, has similarities with western buildings. The prayer hall covered with three domes, is flanked with galleries on three sides. In the interior, a handsome *mihrab* with arches decorated with stalactites is framed by two little columns. The prayer niche opens in the middle of a panel carried out in glazed tiles.

Near the mosque stands a *türbe* comprising a vault under a funerary chamber covered with a dome.

On the slope of the hill, in a quarter which was destroyed by a fire in 1913, there used to be several mosques, among which was the *Settiye Camii*, a former Byzantine church, converted into a mosque in 1117 of which only the apse and a few strips of wall remain.

If we now take the road to Samsun from the central square, we shall see a little beyond the bridge, the *Gümüslüzade Camii* of 1485, then a hospital built in 1308 in the reign of Sultan Olcaitu par Amber, a eunuch of Princess Yildiz.

The richly ornamented portal has an arched niche decorated with stalactites at the back of which a door is cut into a framework of carved stone. The tiercepoint arch of the niche rests on two small engraved columns. The principle façade has two windows with stalactite arches. The portal leads to an entrance hall and a long courtyard flanked, to the right and the left, by a portico under which open out rooms covered with pointed barrel vaults. Opposite is an *iwân* with a Tudor arch flanked by two rooms.

A little further on, the *Memet Paşa Camii* of 1486 is approached by a portico with six bays, and the prayer hall, square in plan, is covered by a dome resting on four pendentives. The minaret has been recessed into the façade at the level of the fourth bay. An inscription above the entrance doorway states that the mosque was founded by Mohammed Pasha, appointed councillor by Beyazit II to Sehzade Ahmet, governor of Amasya.

The road to Samsun crosses the Yeşil Irmak by the Bridge of the Bird and nearby to the right can be seen the domes of the *Beyazit Pasha Camii* preceded by a hostel which must have assured of the revenues of the mosque.

A portico with five bays resting on six columns, faced with alternating rows of yellow and red calcery, has revetments of red and white marble.

Beneath the fourth bay of the portico can be seen a prayer niche and, in the central arch, the door which leads into the prayer hall opens onto a vestibule covered with a dome. As in the Yeşil Camii of Brousse, the prayer hall comprises two bays on different levels and both are covered with a cupola, the first of which also has a lantern.

Notice particularly a little further on, the *Sirvahli Camii* which was only built in 1804 and, at the other end of the Bridge of the Bird, the *Kapi Medresesi* or the *Büyük Ağa Medresesi* of 1488 which is in a very ruinous condition.

We now retrace our steps and continue towards Sivas and after 20 kilometres we pass near the ruins of KALEKOY, a fortress which has existed from remotest times. A tunnelled stairway leads to the fortress constructed on the summit of the hill. Rupestral tombs are carved in the rock.

We then see the ruins of the half buried *Caravanserai of Ezinepazari* established towards 1238 and restored in 1651.

TURHAL, the former Gazioura, a little town on the banks of the Yesil Irmak, lies at the foot of a rocky peak crowned with the ruins of a citadel in which Triarius had established his winter quarters in 68 B.C. during the wars against Mithradates.

Sections of curtain wall are still visible as well as the remains of several towers and two tunnelled stairways.

In the town, the *Ulu Camii*, the Great Mosque, and the *Mahomed Dede Türbesi* of 1301 are not of much interest.

The route continues to follow the valley of Yeşil Irmak and after 20 kilometres, leaves a road to the right for PAZAR, a village near which stands a former Seljuk caravanserai built in 1238 and known by the name of *Hatun Han*. A beautiful portal is surmounted by a broken arch with carved voussoirs and the façade is decorated with geometric motifs with a horseshoe arch resting on two little columns and with two side niches. The other buildings comprise two series of vaulted rooms to the right and to the left of the courtyard as well as a large hall with three aisles.

An old ass-backed bridge not far from here belongs to the Seljuk period.

After having crossed the Yesil Irmak across an old bridge with four broken barrel arches resting on heavy piles reinforced by massive pillars and dating from 1250, we arrive at TOKAT, an important town which extends over the plain and the lower slopes of two cliff-like hills : one, which is formed of two peaks with steep slopes linked by a large causeway, supports the remains of the ancient citadel.

Tokat stands near the site of ancient *Comana* of Pontis and its citadel is the ancient fortress of *Dazimon*. This, with Amaseia, was one of the most important towns of Pontis during the Roman era, but it began to decline during the Byzantine era. After the conquest of Turkey towards the end of the 11th century, the city at the foot of the fortress supplanted the ancient city.

At the entrance of the town to the right we see the *Nur et Tin Sentimur Türbesi*, a mausoleum constructed in 1314 by a Mongol prince. The eastern window is richly decorated and, on the tiercepoint arch which surmounts it, we can read an inscription in the Persian language of verses by the Persian poet Ferdousi.

A little further on and still to the right, stands the *Sünbül Baba Zawiyesi*, a little funerary mosque of 1291 and, again to the right, the façade of the *Gök Medrese*, the Blue Medrese, transformed into a museum and the most interesting monument of the town.

A gate opening at the back of an ogival niche with an arch decorated with stalactites leads into the former theological college which appears to date from the 13th century. The courtyard is surrounded with porticoes on three sides, whilst at the back the walls of the *iwân* are covered with pale blue hexagonal tiles in glazed faience, and with triangular black tiles. Above this revetment runs a band of moulded plaster. The façade of the *iwân* and the arches of the porticoes and galleries are decorated with glazed mosaic of geometric or floral motifs and with panels of geometric decoration carried out in polished brick.

The students' rooms, both on the ground floor and on the first floor, contain antiquities of different periods.

Beyond the Gök Medrese are two caravanserais; the *Vovyoda Han* built towards 1630, and the *Horozoğlu Han* of the 18th century. On the other side of the road, but hidden by houses, is the *Halef Gazi Tekkesi*, a monastery of the end of the 13th century and, in the market place, the *Hatuniye Camii* which has the same attribution as the *Hatuniye Medresesi* of Sultan Beyazit II, has a portico of five arches resting on two antique columns. An inscription above the marble portal, decorated with stalactites, states that the mosque was erected in 1485 by Sultan Beyazit II in honour of his mother Gülbahar Hatun. The vestibule is surmounted by a gallery and the prayer hall by a dome.

We must now look at the *Pasha Hamami*, founded in 1470 by Ali Pasah Camii, a mosque built about 1572 where the broad portico of seven arches precedes the prayer hall covered by a dome on pendentives and, still in the Sulu Sokaği, the *Ebulkasim Türbesi*, of 1235 opposite the *Yağci Hani*, the caravanserai of the oil merchants and, nearby, another caravanserai, the *bedesten* and a little oratory of 1516.

Finally, by keeping to the right, we can see *Ala Mesciti*, an oratory built in 1300 and the *Güdük Minare Camii* of the 15th century.

Incidentally, it is just as well to take note that in these regions where good restaurants are rare that the one at Tokat to the right in the main street is considered to be the best. Its speciality is Shish Kebab with aubergines and potatoes served with wheaten cakes.

We continue on our way to Sivas and, after ten kilometres, we see a steep hill to the left, the Horos Tepesi, crowned by the ruins of an ancient and medieval citadel with a tunnelled staircase and two rock tombs. Thirteen kilometres further on to the right of the road, stands *Ciftlik Han,* a Seljuk caravan-serai of the 13th century, which is partly ruined and then, ten kilometres further on, on leaving the hamlet of Çamlibel, there is another caravanserai of the same period.

The route now becomes mountainous and we cross the pass of Çamlibel, 1,646 metres high, before reaching the township of Yildizeli where we shall find a third caravanserai with the two main bodies of the building separated by a long corridor which was formerly lined with shops installed in the arcades. In the centre of each arcade a door leads, on one side, into a large rectangular hall with four aisles and, on the other, into a smaller room flanked by a mosque and a *hammam*; an inscription indicates that this *hammam* was founded in the 14th century and reconstructed in the 17th.

On crossing the Kisil Irmak we see, to the right, an old ass-backed bridge. We then find ourselves once more on the plain and arrive at SIVAS the ancient *Sebaste* which became Christian as early as the 2nd century. There were many martyrs during the persecutions of Licinius in the 4th century. In the 6th century, Justinian restored the ramparts but this did not prevent the town from being captured in 575 by the King of Persia, Khosroes I. When the emperor Basil II took over from Vaspourakan, the Armenian king, Senekerim Hofhannes received in exchange an important domain in the region of Sebaste which became the capital of this new state. About 40,000 inhabitants from Van followed the king in this exodus which was the prelude to the Armenian migration towards the Mediterranean coast. In 1071 Sebaste was taken by the Turks who then called it Sivas. Then came bands of Norman adven-

turers lead by Roussel de Bailleul who ravaged the interior of
Anatolia, fighting both the Byzantines and the Turks at the
same time. But Roussel, who had allied himself with the former,
was taken prisoner and delivered up to Alexus Comnenus.
Towards the end of the 11th century Sivas became the Capital
of a powerful Danismendides Emirate which included part
of Cappadocia and the ancient province of Pontis. Taken by
the Mongols in the 13th century, it again became the capital
of an independent state, but at the end of the 14th century,
it was handed over to Sultan Beyazit I before being captured
by Tamerlaine who demolished the rampart and massacred
some of the inhabitants. The town declined and continued in
obscurity until the present day.

There are two monuments which justify a visit to Sivas;
the *Gök Medrese* and the *Çifte Medrese*, both remarkable for
their gateways beautifully carved and flanked by two minarets.

We enter the town by the Ismet Pasha Cadese and we see
immediately to the right, at the back of a large empty space,
the two minarets of *Çifte Minare* of which only the façade
remains, all the rooms having been destroyed.

The building of this theological school is attributed to a
Mongol governor who had it erected in 1272. The entrance
opens at the back of a wide niche with a stalactite arch, the
front of which is adorned with marvellous carved decoration
of interlacings and honeycombing in high relief running the
length of three sides with an inscription below. In delicacy
of execution this is one of the most astonishing creations of
Seljuk art. Little columns in the corners of the niche are surmounted by high capitals of acanthus leaves.

On the other side of the gate, are windows or niches framed
with carving in the same style, whilst at the angles, buttresses
show as much imagination and ingenuity in giving variety to
the splendid and perfectly proportioned façade.

Opposite, the *Sifaiye Medresesi*, which is in course of restoration, is a hospital founded in 1217 by the Seljuk Sultan Kay-

mavus I. The gateway, which comprises a great niche with a stalactite vault, has a gate at the back of a recess framed by two borders of delicately carved stone. The tiercepoint arch of the recess is outlined with cable decoration.

We enter into a long vestibule with three rooms on either side. This leads to a courtyard with porticoes which terminate in an *iwân* with rooms on each side. On the right, stands the *türbe* of the Sultan covered with a dome supported by a twelve-sided drum. The façade of the mausoleum is decorated with glazed bricks.

A little further on is the *Mehmet Pasha Camii*, a mosque in the Ottoman style built in 1580, and the *Muzafer Büruciye Medresesi*, a former College of Koranic Theology designed according to the plan of Seljuk *medresesis* with four buildings disposed around a central court. Above the entrance gate an inscription states that it was erected in 1272 during the Mongol period by the vizier Hübedullah Bürucerdcoğlu Muzafer.

The entrance door, in beautiful yellow stone, has a finely carved stalactite niche and, to the right of an entrance hall, there is a little oratory with a *mihrab*, whilst to the left stands the *türbe* of the founder. The columns of the two doors of the courtyard are of Byzantine origin, as well as some of the capitals.

We reach the other remarkable monument of the town through a complicated network of narrow streets. This is the *Gök Medresesi*, the Blue Medrese, former Koranic theological college founded in 1271 by Fahr et Tin surnamed Sahip Atâ who was also responsible for the erection of another *medrese* at Konya. This now houses a little museum.

Like the two other *medreses* of Sivas, contemporary with it, they are distinguished from earlier constructions by the fact that the portal, instead of standing alone on a bare wall, is incorporated into a monumental façade. This latter supported by round buttresses, decorated with interlacing and honey-combing, is pierced with several windows with sculptured frame-

13. BOGAZ KÖY

14. ALACA HOYUK

15. AMASYA

16. SIVAS : GÖK MEDRESE

work. In the centre, the gate opens at the back of a niche with
an arch decorated with stalactities and framed by a portal of
outstanding splendour between the square bases of two minarets
decorated wtih sculpture of geometric character in high relief.
Notice particularly an eight pointed star formed by two squares
of interlocking bricks.

The shaft of each minaret has alternate prismatic and convex
facets separated by little engaged columns constructed of glazed
brick. All the facets are built with turquoise blue or black
glazed bricks forming a network of lozenges.

The front of the portal is formed of carved interlacings and
honeycombing and under the cornice runs a band of inscription.

A fountain to the left is constructed under a niche surmounted by a band of inscription; alternating voussoirs of
yellow limestone and white marble produce a charming
effect.

After passing through an entrance hall with an oratory
decorated with glazed tiles to the right, we come into a courtyard bordered with porticoes to the right and to the left and
terminating in an *iwân* which is now destroyed. Two other
iwâns, with pointed barrel vaulting, have been constructed in
the centre of the side walls. The capitals of the columns of the
doors are of either Seljuk or Byzantine origin.

By means of other narrow streets flanked with picturesque
houses with projecting upper floors, we can go to see the *Ulu
Camii*, the Great Mosque, which is of limited interest.

The prayer hall, rectangular in plan, comprises eleven bays
of ten rows of side columns surmounted by tiercepoint arches
on which rest the rafters. The cylindrical minaret built of bricks
and on an octagonal base has, halfway up, two bands of geometric decoration in polished brick, with an inscription of cufic
characters. Near the top, under a balcony supported by an
encorbelment of stalactites, there used to be another inscription
which is now destroyed. The mosque appears to date from the

end of the 11th century or the beginning of the 12th, and the minaret from the 13th.

From Sivas we can continue towards Kayseri or reach Trebizond or Erzurum by rather unsatisfactory roads.

Those who are not dismayed by bad road conditions and who are making their way towards Erzurum, are advised to make a detour through DIVRIGI so as to see the *Ulu Camii*, with its magnificent portal, as well as the hospital which adjoins it.

But as far as we are concerned, we shall retrace our steps to Amasya and then take the road to Samsun so as to follow the coast of the Black Sea as far as Trebizond.

We return to the Ankara road at Samsun which goes through Navsa before entering the valley of Murat Irmak, then on to Kavak. We can now see, to the right of the road, the *Çakalli Han*, a caravanserai of the 13th century which still has, on the façade of the main room, some beautiful carvings.

We have now come into the Black Sea coastal region where it is often rainy and misty but nevertheless has also long periods of beautiful weather. Even so, the landscape which is still green, contrasts vividly with stretches of burnt-up land stripped of vegetation or completely arid of the kind that we see in Anatolia or along the Mediterranean coast.

The human element is also entirely different; steep and often wooded slopes of the hills and of the mountains of this region shelter a hard-working and dense population which are not without originality and whose distinctive character is in complete contrast to the inhabitants of the rest of Turkey.

We now reach the road from Sinope to Samsun and soon arrive in the latter town, the most important Turkish harbour of the Black Sea.

SAMSUN, the ancient *Amisos*, was founded towards the 7th century B.C. by a colony of Milesians and, after the conquest of Asia Minor by Alexander the Great, it became part of the states of the King of Pontus. During the wars between

Mithridates and the Romans in the 1st century B.C., Amisos
was defeated by General Lucullus and burnt down by the
defenders after the capture of the city. Incorporated into the
Roman Empire, it gradually developed again but suffered from
the competition of the neighbouring port of Sinope. Sacked in
863 by an incursion of the Emir of Malatya, it was taken by
the Seljuk Turks who gave it the name of Samsun.

Burnt down several times during the course of its history,
and notably by the Genoese in 1425, it has not kept a single
monument worth the attention of the tourist. It is today
swiftly developing and gives the impression of a completely
new city.

The road to Trebizond, a little beyond the village, follows
the coast and crosses the alluvial plain of Yeşil Irmak. The
houses, raised at each corner on great blocks of stone to combat
the dampness of the ground, are enclosed in gardens planted
with tobacco. We pass through Çarşamba a little modern town
on the river which the road crosses. We then come to fields
predominantly of maize and the landscape becomes wooded
and has wattle fences and buffaloes which wander along the
road. We get back to the coast and go through the little port
of Terme, ancient *Themiscryra*, before flanking a broad beach
and reaching the town of Unye, where they used to build small
boats.

We then come to the small port of Fatsa, not far from the
ancient *Polemonium* and, after the picturesque hamlet of
Bolaman, the road ascends and following the coast dominates
the sea from a great height before reaching the delightful
village of Yaliköy from which there is a superb view over the
coast.

After passing through a long tunnel, we come out onto the
headland of Cam and we have another splendid view over the
bay of Persembe.

At ORDU we find a reasonably well run hotel. This is
ancient *Cotyora* founded by settlers who came from Sinope

towards the 5th century B.C. It was at *Cotyora* that the sur-
vivors of the celebrated retreat of the 10,000 of Xenophon
embarked for Heraclea of Pontis.

The town is situated at the foot of a green hill and there is
absolutely nothing else of interest except an Armenian basilica
which only dates from the 18th century.

We have now reached the land of the hazelnut which grows
first of all intermingled with maize and then becomes the main
product of Ordu and of Giresun, supplanting other fruit trees
notably the cherry; this tree owes its name to the town of
Kerasos, GIRESUN, which we shall soon pass through.

Giresun spreads over the eastern slope of a promontory
crowned with the ruins of a Byzantine fortress. The ramparts
can still be seen on the edge of the cliff which overlooks the
sea.

Giresun was founded in the 2nd century B.C. by the king
of Pontus, Pharmace, who called it *Pharmacia*. It was known
under the name of *Keresos* when General Lucullus seized it
towards 69 B.C. It was from here that Lucullus took the first
cherry tree into Europe and the tree took the name of the town
from which it came.

As at Ordu, we can see, in an old quarter, a former Armenian
church with a cupola of the 18th century.

As we have mentioned, Lucullus exported the cherry tree,
but the hazel tree was already flourishing in the region at the
time of Xenophon. It was the country of the Mossyneques
whose wooden dwellings, rather like towers, from which their
name (mossyn) has come down to us, have not changed, neither
have the barns on pylons where they store their grain.

In this misty country, where the olive tree does not grow,
the Mossyneques used the oil of the dolphins caught in the
Black Sea, and this continues today to be one of the principle
resources of the fishing hamlets established on the stony penin-
sulas which are unsuitable for vegetation.

After having left Diresun, we catch sight of Diresun Island,

ancient *Aretias*, celebrated in antiquity for its temple which
two Queens of the Amazons, Otrere and Antiope, dedicated
to the god Mars.

Beyond Kesap we have a beautiful view over the coast before
leaving it to cross a magnificent wooded region. From the height
of a short pass, we can see a splendid panorama of the valley
of Yağlidere, to which we now descend by a series of hairpin
bends. We then see, to the left on a rock, the ruins of a fort
which used to defend the entrance to the valley.

We now go through the village of Espiye, surrounded by a
beautiful amphitheatre of wooded mountains, then to Tirebolu,
the ancient Tripolis, which still has, on an islet, the insignificant remains of a Byzantine fortress and of a chapel. The
region which extends to the south was renowned in the days of
antiquity for its silverbearing lead mines.

After Görele, a delightful little township identified as the
ancient *Philocalia*, and Eynesil, not far from the site of ancient
Coralla, we reach the small fishing port of Vakfibekir and here
the climate is different because of the change in the configura-
tion of the coast which is no longer a prey to heavy rain from
the north west. It is no longer damp and the countryside
becomes almost Mediterranean. The hazel trees are confined to
the heights, and near well-tended tobacco gardens, we again
see the olive tree flourishing. Beyond Iskefiye, stone houses with
roofs of round tiles take the place of the wooded houses roofed
with planks.

After the harbour of Iskefiye, we go through Akçaabat,
another little port situated near ancient *Hermonassa*. On a
promontory which overlooks the sea, stands the ruins of a
Byzantine castle built by the Comneni of Trebizond. In the
upper town we find the former church of St Michael now
converted into a dwelling house. It was built in the 13th or
14th century and restored and enlarged in 1846. It comprises
a single nave with a bay preceding the naos covered with a
dome and terminating in an apse which is semi-circular inside

and decorated, on the exterior as well as on the side walls, with little blind arcades.

Further to the south, in the quarter called Orta Mahalle, another church, converted into a chicken house, has preserved, on the right hand wall, remains of frescoes, of which one is a Deisies.

We now arrive in TREBIZOND, and before penetrating into the town we see, to the right, on a terrace, the best-preserved Byzantine monument of the town, the church of Aya Sophia, *Haghia Sophia*.

The terrace on which the church is built used to be bounded to the south with a retaining wall with tombs constructed in semi-circular niches which were painted at the back. Only one of these niches is now visible, and it has a painting of two horsemen, of whom one carries a lance and the other a battle-axe.

The Church of St. Sophia shows a variety of styles : if the construction is in the Byzantine tradition, the characters of the reliefs in the south portal recall Armenian or Georgian decoration, whilst in other parts, Seljuk stalactites and rosettes appear, and some details, like the four lobed windows, are imported from eastern Europe.

Like most of the Byzantine churches of Trebizond, Aya Sofia shows the adaptation from a basilica with three aisles, probably built a little after the beginning of the dynasty of the Comneni of Trebizond in 1204, into a church on the plan of an inscribed cross with a dome. This transformation probably took place in the reign of Manuel I (1238–1263) and it is from this period that the three projecting porches date which were formerly connected by colonnaded galleries. The stalactite capitals of the columns of the north and west porches were added during restoration by the Turks, when they were converting the building into a mosque. The other columns of the porches probably come from monuments of the 5th century. The pediment of the south porch still keeps some of its carved ornamentation

formed of a frieze illustrating the story of Adam who is represented in the right half lying down in the grass, whilst the
Tempter is trying to beguile Eve who then offers the apple
to Adam. These carvings of a rather primitive technique show
Armenian influence.

Above the frieze runs a long inscription in Greek, whilst on
the keystone of the arch above the porch is an eagle with outstretched wings.

Paintings which decorated the interior and which probably
date from the 13th century have recently been discovered.
The powerful action of the figures and the intensity of ex-
pression bring to mind the frescoes of Sopocchani in Yugoslavia,
though it should not be concluded that these paintings have
been influenced by the monumental style in vogue in Salonica
or the art of Constantinople at the end of the 12th century,
or in Nicaea in the first half of the 13th century.

In the church itself, *Christ Pantocrator* is represented on the
dome, whilst the apostles appear between the niches and the
prophets on the blind niches. The frieze above the drum is
decorated with adoring angels. The pendentives are adorned
with pictures depicting *St. Matthew* and *The Crucifixion; St.
John* and the *Descent into Hades; St. Mark* and the *Baptism;
St. Luke* and the *Nativity.*

Above the door which leads to the narthex we find *The Last
Supper, The Washing of the Feet* and *The Agony in the
Garden of Gethsemane*, whilst, near the door which opens onto
the north porch, are *St. Sabas, St. Anthony, St. Euthemios* and
St. Theodosis.

On the arch of the bay which precedes the north apse, we
can see : the *Murder of Zacharius* and the *Flight of Elizabeth,*
in the north apse, the *Visitation* and, near the central apse, the
Annunciation and the *Four Fathers of the Church.*

The central apse still has part of the synthronon and the
seats on several levels which follow the line of the semi-circular
apse. We see the *Doubting St. Thomas*, the *Miraculous Draught*

of Fishes and, in the conch, a *Virgin and Child* between the Archangels Michael and Gabriel, whilst the *Ascension* is depicted on the arch and, on the southern side wall, the *Sending Forth of the Apostles*.

We then go into the south apse and see *The Angels visiting St. Anne*, and *Joachim refusing the offerings in the Temple*. In the side aisle which precedes this apse are depicted the *Birth of the Virgin* and *The Presentation of the Virgin in the Temple*.

In the narthex, which is entirely covered with frescoes, we see, on a central arch a symbolic composition depicting the Gospel, angels, cherubim etc. On the vault of the south bay we see *St. Sergius*, the *Wedding Feast at Cana* and the *Healing of the Paralytic;* on the south wall, the *Miracle of the Boy possessed of a demon*, with his mother imploring Christ to heal him; the child is in contortions as the devil comes out of his mouth.

Above the main door of the narthex, a composition depicts an *Angel adoring the Veil of St. Veronica* and, in the north transept, *Christ Walking on the Waters, Christ Calming the Storm* and *the Healing of the Mother of Peter's Wife*. Above the north door, as well as the figure of Jesus, are what may be members of the Imperial family and in this same bay the *Deisis* and the *Miracle of the Loaves* as well as a portrait of the Virgin.

In the west porch we find the *Last Judgement, Paradise, Hell and the Resurrection of the Dead*, whilst the badly damaged painting in the north porch probably depicts the *Sending forth of the Apostles*, the *Baptism of the Christians, Eight Warrior Saints*, the *Vision of Jacob, Job covered with sores* and the *Tree of Jesse*.

As we can see, this is a complete series which has been uncovered and it is to be hoped that other former Byzantine churches converted into mosques will reveal the frescoes with which they were originally covered once the layers of whitewash have been removed.

Even the original pavement is still visible in certain places, especially under the dome. It is composed of a mosaic of marble of nineteen different varieties. In front of the north porch the foundation of the earlier building has been discovered.

We now cross the suburbs of Trebizond, *Trabzon* in Turkish, and reach the port which is really disappointing. The city itself developed in a most confused way between the sea and the ancient citadel. This latter includes the old quarters which are gradually losing their picturesque aspect.

Trebizond, ancient *Trapezos*, was founded towards the end of the first half of the 1st millennium by Greek colonies from Sinope augmented a little later by an important community from Trapezos in Arcadia. When Xenophon arrived with the 10,000 Greek mercenaries at the end of the 5th century B.C. the population offered sacrifices to Zeus and organized games in honour of the heroes. At peace from the times of the wars between the Romans and Mithridates, the town was occupied by Lucullus, but suffered no damage and kept its status of a free city. It became covered with monuments during Hadrian's time and a second port was artificially hollowed out. Taken by the Goths in 260, it was reconstructed in the Byzantine period and Justinian strengthened the fortifications. In 1204, during the taking of Constantinople by the Crusaders, two sons of the Emperor Andronicus I escaped from the Byzantine capital and took refuge in Trebizond where Alexis Comnenus assumed the title of Emperor and where his successors ruled until 1461. The Comneni held sumptuous court here and formed alliances with the Crusaders, then with the Paleologi but continuing to struggle with the Genoese who wanted to monopolize the Black Sea trade. They were able to repel the assaults of the Seljuk sultans, then of the Mongols and it was not for several years after the fall of Constantinople in 1453 that the last bastion of Byzantine civilization fell to the Turks.

We now arrive in a vast shady square with a 16th-century mosque in the Ottoman style. This is the *Gülbahar Hatun*

Camii with, nearby the *türbe* of the founder, Princess Gülbahar. To the left, a road which leads into the square runs along the eastern side of the Byzantine *enceinte*.

If we continue to follow the main street where we shall find the best restaurant of the town, with a room on the ground floor and a terrace where one can dine in summer, we shall cross the old town which is still surrounded with its ramparts.

The *Fatih Camii*, also called the *Ortahisar Camii*, is none other than the former Byzantine *Church of the Panaghia Chrysocephalos*, the church of the Golden-Headed Virgin now in course of restoration.

It is the most important Byzantine church after Aya Sofia. The entrance is through a porch with two antique columns taken from the southern nave and built by the Turks after its conversion into a mosque. The church, in the form of a Latin cross, is composed of a large nave ending in an apse and flanked by two side aisles surmounted by an upper gallery. A dome resting on a drum surrounded by a balcony covers the crossing of the main aisle and another forming a transept. Just as at St. Sophia, the basilica plan of three aisles was undoubtedly modified in the 13th century by the erection of the dome. At the same time the narthex was raised to the west.

These galleries used to be reached by staircases constructed along the north and south walls; this latter being destroyed during the conversion of the church into a mosque to make way for a *mihrab*. At the top of the northern staircase, we can enter a narrow room without any opening onto the nave, from which we reach the *triforium* by a narrow gallery supported by two columns. Those on the south side have been re-used in the Turkish porch by which the mosque opens to the north. The *triforia*, which open onto the main nave by arcades, used to form the *gynaeceum*. The women could doubtless reach it without crossing the church which would seem to imply that there was another staircase ascending from the narthex.

At one time the dome was faced on the outside with slabs

of gilded bronze which accounts for the name of the church. There is a fountain near the entrance porch, and an ablutions fountain with a marble basin.

It is to be hoped that this former Byzantine cathedral will be deconsecrated like the Aya Sofia and restored to its original state. It formerly had a beautiful floor in Alexandrian work and some panels of mosaic still decorate the apse.

By means of the Kale Sogaği we can reach the upper citadel which we enter by a door cut into the Byzantine *enceinte* constructed in the time of the Comneni. On the outside to the left is a Greek inscription and a Byzantine bas-relief.

We cross the east valley, Takhani Deresi, over a bridge and going also to the right and crossing a popular quarter, we shall reach the *Yeni Cuma Camii*, the former *Church of St. Eugenius* consecrated to the Moslem faith under the name of the new Friday Mosque.

We enter the mosque to the north under a canopy built by the Turks. It has three aisles crossed by a transept, with, at the crossing, a dome resting on a drum pierced with windows and supported by four pendentives resting on four columns of which two are strengthened by a mass of masonry. The three aisles each terminate in an apse. As the pilaster engaged in the southern wall does not support anything, we must deduce that the church has been converted, doubtless after the fire which damaged it in 1340. The addition of a central dome results in the enlargement of the central aisle, the former sanctuary having been planned like the preceding one on the design of a basilica with three aisles.

We now get back to the main street, Uzun Yolu, where we can see in a narrow side street the *Zeytinkik Camii*, a much ruined former Byzantine church of the 13th or 14th century of which nothing remains but the apse with three semi-circular bays.

We should notice also, in the Maras Cadesi a little before crossing the eastern valley, to the left of the former church of St. Anne, the oldest Christian sanctuary of Trebizond. It comprises three aisles ending in semi-circular apses. The four columns which separate the three aisles are of ancient origin and surmounted by imposts and Ionic capitals. The very much defaced inscription which runs above the south door gives the date as 884 to 885. It was in fact built during the reign of Basil I (867–886) and it is over a crypt which is inaccessible.

Do not bother to visit the *Church of St. Basil* on the other side of the road. After having served as a shop, it collapsed and was razed to the ground. The columns dated from the Roman epoch or the early years of the Byzantine era.

In this quarter, we shall also find the *Nakip Camii*, a former church with three aisles terminating in projecting apses. This may have been the *Church of St. Andrew* who, according to tradition, is said to have introduced Christianity into Trebizond. Built with antique materials, especially the central apse, this church, which today is almost in ruins, probably dates from the 10th or 11th century.

It is worth mentioning two other ruined churches in the north quarter, one which only dates from the 18th century, the other, in a private garden, goes back to the time of the Comneni but may have been restored during Ottoman times.

In the eastern quarter, not far from the road to Erzurum, the former *Church of St. Philip*, which became the Greek cathedral after the confiscation of the Palageo Chrysthanos, was in its turn seized in 1665. According to the Metropolitan Chrysanthos, it was erected by a daughter of Alexis III Comnenes (1349–1390).

It is composed of a short transept, a *naos* covered with a dome, and a deep apse. It was enlarged during its conversion into a cathedral.

In the same direction, three kilometres from the town by the Erzurum road, the *Kaymakli Monastiri* is a former Armenian monastery which was occupied by monks until just after the First World War. To the left of the entrance, in the courtyard, we find the ruins of an isolated belfry. The church, which has lost its roof, was founded in the 15th or 16th century and restored several times. We can find traces of paintings carried out in the 18th century on top of older ones; a chapel dates from 1622.

Another monastery, *Theoskepastos*, on the slopes of Boz Tepe to the east of the town, described by Millet in 1894, is now in ruins and the underground chapels of Saint Savas decorated with 15th-century paintings on the upper side are now inaccessible.

We shall now turn our steps towards Erzurum by a highway which climbs up the green valley of Değirmendere. It is an itinerary which shows us the contrast between the wooded vegetation of the shores of the Black Sea, with its hazel trees, cherry trees and forests, and the steppes of the high mountain plateaus.

After 18 kilometres we leave, on the left, a picturesque ass-backed bridge, and then go on to Esiroglu and to Macka. It is a little longer than the road to the left but gives us a chance to go through Meryemana where we can visit the *Monastery of Sumela*, which is now abandoned.

Situated at an altitude of 1,200 metres on the slope of a cliff which dominates the valley from about 300 metres away, this monastery dedicated to the Virgin, is built on a narrow ridge. According to legend, it was founded in the 6th century in the time of Justinian, but most of the buildings date from the Comneni of Trebizond; Emperor Alexis III was crowned there in 1340.

The only entrance to the monastery at the end of a steep stairway leads into a building which contains the porter's lodge. We then go down by a staircase into the principle court-yard, passing on our right a building constructed in 1860 to house visitors. To the west the courtyard is surrounded by a church constructed in a grotto, a chapel and several monastery buildings. The entrance to the grotto is closed by a wall decorated with frescoes which adjoins the chapel, erected in 1710 and decorated with paintings executed in 1740 during the restoration of the monastery. The side walls of the main church are covered with paintings of the 14th century and Alexis III is represented in one of them between Manuel III and Andronica. The ones on the north wall, which are quite well preserved, are also 14th century; the others, very much blackened, date from the restoration of 1740.

The courtyard to the north west is surrounded by various monastery buildings and three little chapels. The sections built on the edge of the ridge which becomes narrower and narrower were erected in the 17th century. A room to the north cut into the cliff side must have been a library.

At the foot of the monastery a second building dates only from the 19th century.

We then go to Küçük Konak from which we can reach, after two or three hours on foot, the *Monastery of St. John*, called Vazelon. The church is quite recent but a chapel has kept a few traces of paintings.

We reach the first forests which cover the slopes of the mountain of the western chain and then come to the pass of Zigana, 1,975 metres high. At Torul we see, to the left, on a rocky peak, the remains of a fortress. The highway then crosses a gorge before coming out onto the high plateau where we discover beyond an old ass-backed bridge the little town of GÜMÜSHANE. Of this former Byzantine city, 7 kilometres away, some old dwellings remain as well as some Byzantine churches where frescoes have recently been uncovered; a cathedral, several mosques, among them the *Suleymaniye Camii* of the 16th century and some Turkish baths.

We now come to the little village of Kale dominated by a rocky peak crowned with the ruins of a medieval fortress and, after having gone over the pass of Vavuk, 1,900 metres high, we arrive at BAYBURT, an important garrison town situated at the foot of a fortress reconstructed by the Turks, but which still keeps, notably on the north front, vestiges of ramparts which are earlier than the Seljuk conquest. They probably date from the Armenian period at the time when the Bagratide kings possessed a castle in this region.

We find in the main road a restaurant where we can lunch before going towards the pass of Kopdağt 2,400 metres high, after which a magnificent panorama opens out over the mountain of Palandoken and of Karagapazan. A belfry erected on an Armenian church sounds the alarm to warn travellers as soon as the wind rises, because the sudden storms here are exceptionally violent.

We then find at Oskale another medieval fortress in ruins before rejoining the road to Erzincan and to Sivas and we drive across the high plateau to Erzurum.

ERZURUM, 1,905 metres high, has a rough climate in winter and even in spring. It is still cold in summer. The city did not gain importance until the Byzantine era. Under the name of *Theodosiopolis* it became, after Armenia was abandoned to the Persians between 387 and 390, one of the principle Byzantine strongholds of the eastern provinces of the empire. In 633 the Byzantines held a synod here in the course of which it imposed on the Armenian church the principle of attachment to the Greek Orthodox Faith. The Imperial forces, beaten by the Arabs in Armenia, lost the city in 655 but retook it in 657. Lost again, it was retaken yet once more in 751 by Constantine V and then destroyed and evacuated and the population transferred to Thrace. Seized in 928 by the Arabs and governed by an Armenian in 978 it became part of the Bagratide kingdom of Tayq, the mountainous region which we have just crossed. It was called *Karin*. The Turks reoccupied the city in 1071 and called it Arz er Roum, the land of the Romans, from which came the name Erzurum. According to an Arab traveller, the city was already very much ruined in the 14th century.

As we enter the city, we shall see to the left the minaret of the *Yakutive Medresesi* built in 1311 by Hoca Yakut in the reign of a Mongol king of Persia, Il-Khân Oldjâïtou Khodâbendeh which is occupied by the army and has a very beautiful sumptuously carved porch. It is on the same plan as the *Çifte Minare Medrese* which we shall see later, but it is on a smaller scale. The minaret is superbly proportioned.

We then pass a little Seljuk *türbe* before finding, to the right, the most remarkable group of buildings in the city. The *Ulu Camii*, the Great Mosque, is in course of reconstruction, and contains seven great aisles with a dome above the transept of the niche of the *mihrab* and the *Çifte Minare Medrese.*

The *medrese* has two minarets which rival those we have seen at Sivas and a former Koranic theological college founded in 1253 by the Seljuk Sultan Ala et Tin Kaykobat.

The façade has an arched portal decorated with stalactites flanked by two grooved cylindrical minarets on high bases. Two broad bands of carving frame the portal and two motifs in high relief decorate the bases of the two minarets, whilst on each side of the door, a double headed heraldic eagle surmounts palm leaf *motifs*. Semi-cylindrical buttresses are placed near the corners.

Inside a courtyard with four *iwâns* (the one at the back has disappeared) is surrounded by a double row of galleries. Some of the columns have richly decorated capitals and we should also notice the tiercepoint decoration of the arch of the north *iwân* resting on two columns.

The *medrese* is now used as an archaeological museum.

Behind the *medrese* we see the tall silhouette of *Hatuniye Türbesi* erected by the daughter of Ala et Tin Kaykobat in 1255 to serve as his mausoleum. The dedicatory inscription was carried off by the Russians during the course of the war of 1828. It is the most graceful building decorated with blind arches and covered with a dome surmounted by a pyramid roof and lighted by several windows with stalactite pediments.

A little further behind we can see, in a large space surrounded by a little wall, three other *türbes* also circular and decorated with blind arcades. The most remarkable is the *Emir Sultan Türbesi* erected during the Seljuk period in the 12th century. Designed on an hexagonal plan, it is decorated on each face, with the exception of the one with the entrance door, by a double niche in a rectangular frame. The upper part on a circular plan has a broad cornice with stalactites. The reliefs which decorate the niches depict symbolic figures of serpents, heads of eagles, rabbits, etc.

From the other side of the main road we shall reach the old castle with a clock tower erected in the 19th century on the foundation of a Seljuk corner tower. The walls of the citadel are very well preserved with a double entrance door and, in the interior, the *enceinte* of *Gümüghu Türbe*, a mausoleum which is also of the Seljuk period. We shall find other *türbes* at Erzurum like the *Karanlik Türbe* erected in the 13th century by the Seljuk Emir Sadr et Tin and the *Ali Baba Türbesi* which is also of the 13th century, etc.

H

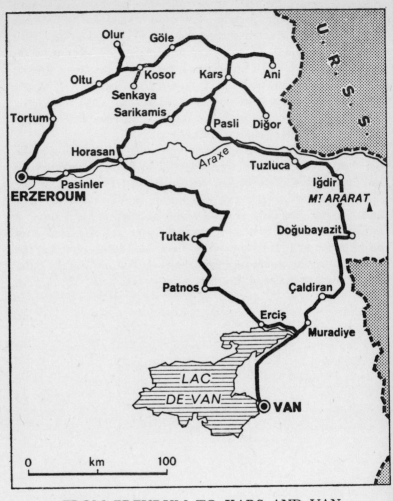

FROM ERZURUM TO KARS AND VAN

ITINERARY IV

FROM ERZURUM TO KARS AND TO VAN

Haho — Oltu — Penek — Kars — Ani —
Horomos — Khtzgonk — Digor — Tuzluca
Doğubayazit — Agri — Ercis — Van — Toprakkale

ALTHOUGH the direct highway from Erzurum to
Doğubayazit is surfaced, the others are mainly rough
gravelled. They are sometimes impassable after a land-
slide following a storm, or dangerous because of the Kurdish
bandits who roam in this area. It is also preferable, at Kars, to
come back to Horasan and to drive via Agri to get to Dogubayazit; also there is something to be said for returning to Agri
to get to the lake of Van. We will now explore the various
alternatives.

We leave Erzurum by the road to Horasan which, after 39
kilometres, goes through Pasinler, the principal township of
Akaza near which we can see, not far from the village of
Kazankale, a ruined fortress founded by the Armenians and
restored by Uzun Hasan.

At Horasan we take to the left the road for Kars after looking
at a beautiful bridge which crosses the Araxe, and which was
constructed in the 16th century by the architect Sinan to whose
genius we owe the existence of the most beautiful mosques in
Turkey.

This route follows a most picturesque gorge flanked by
mountains of a fascinating diversity of shapes. The valley
broadens out into a wide plain. This route is an easy one;

unfortunately it offers no archaeological interest, and there is only the Armenian castle of MECINBERT which we can see beyond Andereköy, and the Armenian church of ÇANGILI beyond Karakust.

On the other hand we shall see several most interesting Armenian buildings by taking the road through Tortum. It first crosses a marshy depression before rising up again by way of the Gürcü Boğazi along the valley of the Georgians as far as the pass of Akcor which is 43 kilometres away. The country-side changes and we find in the Plain of Çoruh abundant waters and rich, well-cultivated valleys.

We now descend rapidly, following the right bank of Tortum Tay as far as the military post of TORTUM at 1,600 metres altitude. Down below we can reach in about two hours on foot the village of Tortum Kane, former capital of the valley dominated by a ruined Georgian castle. A little further on, at the 74th kilometre, we go up again to the left, the valley of Vankderesi and after three hours of walking, reach the beauti-ful 10th-century *Church of Ekek*.

We then arrive at Vihik Hapisi, a little group of houses on the edge of the river, from which by a track, negotiable by cars, in spite of an awkward ass-backed bridge over the Tortum Çay, we reach the village of HAHO (Khakouli) at 1,500 metres altitude. Here we find a remarkable monastic group. To begin with, the 10th-century *Church of the Mother of God* founded by David the Great of Takik. It is on the plan of a large domed basilica. It is very well preserved and has remarkable archaic carvings representing fantastic animals borrowed from Iranian bestiaries and figures of saints or biblical characters such as Jonah. The apse has the remains of paintings and we can still see the 9th-century chapel of David as well as a number of chapels scattered over the mountainside.

Instead of continuing to Osk and Artirim, we return to the 68th kilometre where we shall take to the right the road which goes up the valley of the Ahpusor to continue over the

Pass of the same name to an altitude of 2,250 metres and then descend once more into the valley of Sivridere with its multi-coloured rocks. We reach OLTU, ancient Oukhthik, capital of the province of Taik and residence of the Georgian princes. It is 1,300 metres high on the banks of the Oltu Çay and is dominated by a well-preserved castle on a rocky peak a little beyond the town which has an Armenian church in its *enceinte*.

We then leave, 17 kilometres further on, the road which leads to OLUR in a region which is unfortunately difficult of access but where there are a large number of Georgian churches and castles. Alas, we cannot get to them without hours of very difficult walking.

Further on, the valley of Kanlieu is crossed by a negotiable track along the right bank. After two kilometres, there is to the right the famous *Church of Penek* (Bana) built by Prince Adarnase II (881–923). It is on a four lobed plan surrounded by two circular naves pierced with semicircular windows. The colonnade of the apse is most remarkable. The building suffered much damage during the Russo-Turkish war of 1877.

Two kilometres further on, we shall see another church, central in plan; *Harap Kilise* (Kadjus tzihe) which is a little later in date.

From here, by a steep climb of two hours we reach SAĞOMANKALE where we shall find a castle with a chapel decorated with frescoes and a rock church which is also covered with frescoes of the 11th century.

The route to Kars then goes through Kosor from which we can reach SANKAYA 15 kilometres to the south. Near this village we can visit the little three-aisled *Church of Ortülü*.

The road then crosses the plateau of Göle and reaches Kars after a run of about 269 kilometres instead of 225 by the other itinerary. KARS which was an important town during the Armenian period from the 8th to 11th century was occupied at the end of the 9th century by the Emir Afsin, Turkish governor of Azerbaidjan under the Califs of Bagdad. Retaken by the Armenians, it became the seat of the Bagratide dynasty in the reign of Ashot II (914–929) and acquired splendid monuments during the reign of his successor Abas (929–953). King Ashot III Olomada transferred his capital to Ani and gave Kars to his brother Moushel who, in his turn, in 962, took the title of King. Besieged unsuccessfully in 1055, the town was linked up again in 1064 to the Seljuk Sultanate of Persia, but retaken in 1205 by a Georgian army and incorporated into the kingdom of Georgia. After the Ottoman conquest of 1514, Kars became an important stronghold near the Turko-Russian frontier and was besieged again and again by the Russians who occupied it between 1878 and 1920.

The town is dominated by the citadel constructed in the 11th century on the site of a fortress of the Seljuk period which was destroyed by the Russians during the Crimean War, then rebuilt in the 19th century. The inner citadel is on a peak of trachyte encircled by the river. Halfway up the slope, the upper town was protected by a wall; all that remains are vestiges of the later period—a *medrese*, the *Ulu Camii*, the *Beglerbegi sarayi*. The lower town at the foot of the escarpment, was bounded by another rampart flanked with towers and pierced with gates which disappeared in the modern building development. A school has just been disastrously constructed quite close to the citadel.

It is at the foot of the citadel that we can see the most remarkable building of Kars; the *Church of the Holy Apostles*, a former Armenian church erected in the 11th century by a Bagratide king and now transformed into a museum.

It is a church with a dome erected on a square plan with four radiating apses semi-circular in the interior, but polygonal on the exterior. The dome is surmounted by a cylindrical cone resting on a deep drum decorated with twelve blind arches, above which are twelve reliefs depicting the twelve apostles. Adapted into a mosque after the Turkish conquest, it was reconsecrated to the Christian faith between 1878 and 1920 and since then has been considerably altered.

The modern town comprises an entire quarter built by the Russians at the end of the 19th century in the style of that country with a cathedral adapted as an electric power house.

If Kars has no great interest to offer us, there are many Armenian buildings in the neighbourhood, but as it is along the frontier zone it is essential to obtain a pass from the police in particular to go and see the remains of the town of Ani. An official will come with you in your car and see that your permit is stamped at two military posts. The route to Ani goes across a high fertile plateau where corn and oats flourish; enormous groups of cows, goats and sheep roam over rich pastures. Here and there are a few villages with black stone houses thatched with straw.

The track is relatively good apart from some more difficult stretches and at the end of an hour and a half one can see the outline of the walls of the ancient Bagratide capital.

ANI may have been founded at the beginning of the 9th century in the reign of Ashot II (806–827) who was a member of the royal family of the Bagratides. In the reign of Ashot III Olomadz (953–957) it became the Bagratide capital. In 961 Ashot III was anointed king at Ani by the Patriarch Ananias and soon afterwards a strong rampart was built round the town. It was during the course of a council held at Ani in 969 that the Patriarch Vahan I, successor of Ananias—a partisan of the reunion of the Armenian and Byzantine church—was deposed and replaced by Stephanos III of Sevan.

Sembat II (977–990) improved the town and in the course of eight years protected it by a double rampart reinforced with round or rectangular towers. In 989, the building of the cathedral was taken in hand under the direction of the architect Terdat who finished it in 1001 in the reign of Gagik I (990–

1020). In 993, the seat of the patriarch of Armenia was transferred from Arkina to Ani. The successor of Gagik I, Hovhannes Sembat (1020–1039) had to fight against his brother Ashot IV supported by the Byzantine and the Ardzrounian Seneqerim Hovhanes of Vaspourakan. He was obliged to cede vast territories of his realm to his brother and, to add to his troubles, the King of Georgia, Giorgi I (1014–1027) pillaged Ani, took him prisoner and only freed him on payment of a high ransom.

Threatened by the Seljuks, he thought it salutary to place himself under the protection of Byzantium, but he made the mistake of promising Basil II that his kingdom would revert to the Empire after his death. Then when he did die in 1041 a Byzantine army marched on Ani in order to insist upon the terms of the promise, but the Armenian nobility under the leadership of Vahran Pahlavouni took up the cause of the nephew of the dead man. The Byzantine troops were cut to pieces and the young Gagik II was crowned king of Ani in 1042. Basileus Constantine Monomacus sent two new armies to seize the kingdom of Ani, and in 1044 sent the Emir of Dovin to march against the town.

Gagik II, having made the mistake of going to Constantinople to the court of the Emperor to sign a treaty of allegiance, was forced to renounce the sovereignty of his kingdom and in 1045 the Byzantines made their entry into Ani, but from 1048 they had to repulse an attack by the Seljuk Turks and in 1055 it was the Emir of Dovin who ravaged the surroundings of the town without daring to besiege it. However, less than twenty years after the forced cession of the kingdom of Ani to the Byzantines, the town was taken by Alp Arslan. The Armenians in despair believed they had been betrayed by the Byzantines. It was only during short intervals that the town was seized back from the Moslems. In 1124 Danith II, King of Georgia, recaptured Ani which he gave as a fief to the Armenian family of the Zakharides who were only able to hold it for two years.

In 1153, the Georgians defeated beneath the walls of the city the troops of the Emir of Erzurum but they were not able to capture Ani until 1162 and then they finally lost it in 1165. Giorgi III (1156–1184) managed once more before the end of his reign to seize back Ani from the Moslems. The Armenian governors of Ani were to remain under the sovereignty of the Georgians until the Mongol invasions towards the middle of the 13th century. Then the town was gradually depopulated and was soon after abandoned.

It is therefore a dead city which we discover in an extra-ordinary site, a sort of peninsula between two deep ravines which come together to encircle a fortress at the far end. A strong wall links the two ravines and it is this rampart which we see at first with its doube *enceinte* built of either golden yellow or salmon pink stone with warm tones. If the exterior towers are for the most part broken down, the interior towers seem almost intact in spite of the cracks which show on some of them. There are bastions as massive as keeps and some are round and most impressive, such as those which defend the Alparqlan Kapisi, the main gate, which still has the bas-relief representing a rampant lion. The gate of Kars, *Çifte beden Kapi*, is also flanked by two large round towers, while to the left, 300 metres away, the gate *Hidirellez Kapi* has a curious chequered decoration of the Georgian period.

We then see, a little further on, the towers of Chanouche and of Mamahatoun of the 13th century decorated with a bull's head with two serpents. This is the emblem of Vatchou-tanz family who governed Ani on behalf of the Georgians.

Within the walls, a huge space, almost flat, is covered with wild plants and bushes punctuated here and there by more or less ruined monuments, with in the background, the fortress, which dominates the confluence of the two rivers.

We begin by following the interior of the *enceinte* to reach the two churches which are furthest to the left. The first one is the *Church of the Redeemer*, begun in 1034 by King

Hovhanes Sembat to contain a fragment of the True Cross,
but restored and redesigned several times. Some years ago this
building split in two and it is now in a state of ruin.

It is a circular building which was surmounted with a dome
which gives it an oriental aspect. The deep drum rests on
eight supporting niches. It was doubtless badly balanced because it had to be restored several times. On the outside, the
base and the drum of the dome are decorated with blind
arcading with slender columns and the semicircular arches
which are one of the characteristics of Armenian architecture
and more particularly of the religious buildings which we shall
see at Ani. We can make out the interior remains of frescoes
of the 13th century.

We now arrive at the *Church of St. Gregory of Tigrane
Honentz* which stands 200 metres to the south east near a
rampart and dominates the deep canyon of the Arpa çay
which now serves as a frontier between Turkey and the
USSR.

It is an important building in the form of an inscribed cross
with, in the centre, a dome resting on a deep drum. It is preceded by a narthex which is partly destroyed but keeps one of
its lateral walls and the arcade extending beyond the entrance
porch resting on elaborate capitals.

On the outside the drum of the dome as well as the walls
are decorated with blind arcading with slender columns where
the semi-circular arch is delicately carved. Amidst foliage and
garlands the animal figures are very beautiful in style and face
or follow each other : cocks, pheasant, eagles, peacocks, stags,
hares, bears, ibex, dragons. These are in the Iranian manner
such as can be seen more particularly on the ivory coffers of
the period.

The interior is entirely covered with paintings, which deal
on the western arm, with a history of the apostolate of St.
Gregory the Illuminator, who converted the Armenians and
their king Tiridates. Each of these scenes, painted on a beautiful

royal blue background of the Sassanid tradition, bear a
Georgian inscription; scenes of the Gospels and figures of saints
and apostles decorate the other arms.

There we can see how Tiridates, before his conversion, had
Ripsime and her companions decapitated because the young
virgin had resisted his advances; how he martyred Gregory
who refused to recant and how, when sick, he went in search
of the saintly man. The rest depict baptism of pagans and the
ordination of priests.

We go up to the plateau again in order to see the most
impressive religious building of Ani—the *Cathedral* which
was built by an Armenian named Tiridates between 989 and
1010 for the king Sembat II, then for his daughter-in-law
Queen Catramides. It is built in the same basalt and trachyte
which gives so much character to the buildings of Ani, distribu-
ting at random, brown and pink stone which does not destroy
the unity but adds an iridescent touch.

Pillaged by the Turks who transformed it into a mosque
in 1064, it was restored by the Georgians at the beginning of
the 13th century, then converted into a caravanserai before
being completely abandoned. The dome has collapsed, but
apart from the porches which have been destroyed, the different
façades are more or less intact.

On the outside, there is the same decoration of blind arcading
with long, narrow windows similar to loopholes and a restrained
decoration beneath the arches.

The interior is the same, but devoid of decoration with its
huge nave flanked by two narrow aisles, the pillars of the dome
with elegant little columns and the choir with the slightly
pointed and decorated arch in its lower section and niches in
the blind arcading.

Different inscriptions mention the construction and the
various restorations, the last dating from 1486.

From the cathedral we go on to the *Monastery of the Virgin*
which is to be found, like St. Gregory of Tigranes, on the edge

of the canyon. It is a hexagonal church of the 13th century below which can be distinguished remains of an Armenian bridge which spanned the Arpa çay.

We now direct our steps towards the extremity of the peninsula which was barred by the ramparts of the original town, the ramparts of Ashot III, of which we can still see the foundation of the great round towers in red stone. To the left on the edge of the canyon rises up the *Mosque of Menoutcher* built in 1072 by the first Moslem governor of the town. A tall hexagonal minaret of brown and golden stone stands beside a beautiful vaulted hall with massive red columns of definite Armenian character. From the windows of the mosque there is a superb view over the ravine and the plateaux of the other bank in Russian territory.

We then see another mosque in ruins which bears a bilingual inscription in Persian and in Armenian dated 1198. It says that the sale of camels and of sheep was forbidden in front of the religious building, which reminds us that Ani was an important commercial city on the caravan route coming from India and Persia and going towards Trebizond and Anatolia.

There still remain from the Moslem period the walls of the palace and, more particularly, an entrance decorated in a mosaic of stone tiles in the Iranian style which may be of the 11th or 13th century.

We then go on to the ruins of the little *Church of Achot* and climb up to the citadel or *kale* which contains the *Church of the Palace*. This is a little basilica with a nave of polychrome stones, partly collapsed, where one can still see very beautiful capitals of the 7th and 8th century decorated with rather rough carving representing more particularly : birds, an eagle on a wounded deer, and the Sacrifice of Abraham. It may have been founded in 622 by a Kamsarakan prince.

Below, to the south east, the *Mausoleum of the Princely Children* of the 10th century is quite well preserved as well as the steep spur of the escarpment which dominates the meeting of the canyons, the *Kiz Kale*, a little hexagonal chapel of the 9th and 13th century, one of the prototypes of the church with radiating chapels and a dome. It is preceded by a rectangular narthex and the drum of the dome is decorated in the interior with blind arcading.

We shall visit, after returning from the walls, the *Church of St. Gregory Aboughamrentz* which goes back to the middle of the 10th century and which is also typical of the circular churches on a radiating plan with six supporting niches, a dome on a twelve-sided drum on the exterior.

The *Church of the Holy Apostles* which dated from 1031 is unfortunately ruined with the exception of the narthex of the Mongol period. It is a great hall with a dome with powerful ribs in tiercepoint, a sumptuously decorated portal in the Iranian style and a stalactite niche. This edifice, which dates from the 13th century, was intended for civil use for it is covered with inscriptions of the 13th and 14th centuries concerned with taxes. Another of 1303 indicates that the relics of a hermit interred here can heal every malady.

We then pass in front of the *Church of St. Gregory of Gagik*, founded by king Gagik I (989–1020), in imitation of the famous church of Zwartnotz now in Russian Armenia and which dates from the 7th century. Circular in plan like its model, it was badly balanced, for it collapsed some years after its erection; several beautiful basalt capitals in the Archaic style slid to the ground.

Let us notice the remains of several palaces : those of the *Palace Paranof* of the 12th and 13th centuries with a pretty façade of two storeys with a graceful window; those of the *Palace Medjed Manouche* of the 11th century with its remains of stalactites and its hall with low, massive columns supporting the heavy semi-circular arches.

It is a complex of admirable monuments which should be saved from permanent ruin; why should not the Gulbenkian foundation, which has just given considerable sums for the restoration of Armenian monuments in Soviet Russia, interest itself in the Armenian churches of Ani?

Other Armenian buildings are worth seeing in the neighbourhood of Ani and first of all, the MONASTERY OF HOROMOS which is 15 kilometres away to the north east. It can be reached by a reasonable track which follows the Arpa çay. It was the pantheon of the Kings of Armenia. First of all we pass the *Church of the Shepherd*, an interesting building on the plan of a star, then in front of the ruins of a triumphal arch under which Royal processions used to pass. We go down into the ravine of the Arpa çay and in a desolate bend we find the remains of two little churches, *St. Menas* of the 10th century and *St. George* of the 11th century, graceful little chapels with the brown stone rising up in the midst of green grass not far from a bubbling spring. A third chapel which has collapsed used to contain the tomb of Ashot III the Charitable.

A little further on, on a hill, stands the great *Monastery of St. John* which was founded in the 10th century by Armenian priests from Byzantine lands. Burnt by the Moslems in 982, it was soon rebuilt and it was then that it became the Pantheon of the kings of Ani. An inscription of the beginning of the 11th century states that King Sembat III gave the taxes of a certain village for the upkeep of the tombs. Even though these are dilapidated we can still see the magnificent headstones which rise up behind them. It is in a great vaulted hall which opens onto the southern side of the church where we shall find four Royal *hatchkars* with the gorgeous outlines of the Armenian crosses, whilst sumptuous decorative oriental inscriptions spread over the wall.

The church, on the plan of an inscribed cross with a central dome, is preceded by a narthex larger than the main body of the building and divided into three aisles by massive stocky pillars supporting heavy semi-circular arches. The coffered ceiling decorated with crosses and rosettes and the interior of the drum of the bell turret with columns above the centre of the narthex remind us that it is to Central Asia that we should look for the origins of Armenian art. Bunches of grapes, pomegranates and different motifs which make one think of Persian rugs decorate the whole interior of the bell turret and plunge us into an oriental fairyland.

In contrast, on the exterior, the drum of the dome of the church is entirely plain, whilst the door is soberly framed by two linked columns surmounted above a semi-circular arch with a narrow window cut out of a large elaborately carved panel.

Besides the funerary chambers we have already described, we have still to see the Hall of the Synod with ogival arches and, if the church was built in 1038 by King John Sembat, later buildings of the 13th century are due to the governors of Ani of the period. The monastery remained an important centre of Armenian civilization until the 18th century and consequently survived for several centuries after the ruin of Ani.

In the middle of the last curves just before the village of Digor or Tekor we leave the road to descend on foot into the canyon opening up to the right. After half an hour we come to the MONASTERY OF KHTZGONK or Beskilise. There we see a magnificent complex of five principle churches mainly dating from the 11th century: *St. Stephanos, St. Sarkiss, St. Karapet,* and the *Church of the Virgin* are grouped together; two are even back to back whilst the *Church of the Illuminator* stands a kilometre away. One of these is circular, on two storeys built of beautiful yellow stone and surmounted by a ribbed dome like the characteristic one of Zwartnotz; two others are back to back and one of these has a plain drum like St. John's of Horomos and the other has an octagonal drum.

Only the foundations remain of the celebrated 5th-century *CHURCH OF DIGOR.*

By taking very difficult tracks we can also drive 50 kilometres to the south-west to KARABAG where the *Church of Mren,* a domed basilica of the 7th century has walls decorated with important carvings of figures.

It is worth noticing finally, 20 kilometres to the west of Ani, near the village of Kozluca, reached by a track which is difficult for cars, the MONASTERY OF BAGNAIR from the 10th and 13th centuries, and two hours' walk to the south west of Ani near the canyon of Arpa çay which it dominates, the CASTLE OF MAGAZBERT. It is in an almost perfect state of preservation and an excellent example of Armenian military architecture of the 10th century.

To return from Kars to Van, we again have the choice of two routes; the shortest and the most picturesque is the one which goes through Tuzluca and Mt. Anarat and rejoins Dogubayazit, but it is a mountainous route and, in sections, only mediocre. Here is a brief description of it : we first take, after 23 kilometres, the road to Erzurum, then we cut across to the left and reach the valley of the Araxe. At Pasli a valley which opens out to the left enables us to reach, 6 kilometres away, KECIVAN which is to be found on the site of the former Armenian town of Artageyra but only Seljuk monuments, a castle, a mosque and a *kumbet* with a beautiful sculptured portal are left.

We then come to TUZLUCA. It is to the north west of the village on the right bank of the Çildir çay, a tributary of the Araxe, and shall find the former Armenian town of BAGARAN which was the residence of the Bagratide Ashot the Great (856–890) in the 9th century. The excavations near the frontier are difficult of access. Here we can see a church constructed between 624 and 631 on a central plan with four radiating apses.

We then come to Igdir, still following the valley of the Araxe, and flanking the Russian frontier. This little township of more than 12,000 inhabitants is situated at an altitude of 850 metres at the foot of the massive of Ararat which stands out very well. It is from this point that it is easiest to scale.

Mt. Ararat, Ağri Daği, is a volcano with a summit attaining 5,156 metres, which last erupted on 20th June 1840. We know that according to tradition it was upon Mt. Ararat that Noah's Ark landed after the flood.

From Igdir a track which goes through the village of Basköy leads to the valley of Ahira at the entrance to which we can see a group of five crosses carved in the rock and, a little higher up, a number of grottoes which were occupied by anchorites. Higher still one is shown the spring which Jacob caused to gush forth to slake the thirst of his companions when they came onto the ridge to the places where Noah's ark may have grounded. Three thousand metres higher up, we come to a heavily crevassed glacier and a number of little lakes with jets of sulphurous gas on the surface. Cones of yellow, black or red tufa also remind us that we are on a volcano.

At a level of 4,000 metres we reach the lake of Kor with, on a terrace below the little fortress of *Koran Kilise*, and the ruin of an Armenian church.

We then leave the muddy plain of Araxe to go over the pass of Cengel and we arrive at DOĞUBAYAZIT, a township situated on the road from Erzurum to Tabriz, an excellent surfaced road at the foot of a spur dominated by the ruins of a citadel founded, it is said, in the first millennium B.C. in the time of the Kingdom of Ourartu.

Almost at the summit of the spur, an enormous Assyrian relief with a vannic inscription in cuneiform characters is carved. On the other side of the river, following the foot of the hill on which stands the fortress built in the Seljuk period, there comes into view, like a fairy stage set, the spectacular ruins of a palace erected at the end of the 17th century by Isak Pasha who was of Kurdish origin and to whom is also attributed the mosque called *Isak Pasha Camii*, in which there is a delightful mingling of Seljuk, Armenian and Georgian styles.

The prayer hall on a square plan is surmounted by a dome above a terrace.

It is also possible to set out from Doğubayazit to make the ascent of Mt. Ararat which does however offer greater difficulties.

From Doğubayazit a road goes directly to the region of Lake Van if it is not cut by landslides. It leads to ÇALDIRAN, a village dominated by a hill where a little fortress of the Ourartu period has been found of which traces of the *enceinte* are still visible.

It was near this village that, in 1514, Sultan Selim I beat the King of Persia, Ismail I.

We then go to MURADIYE where, beneath the foundations of a castle erected towards 1500 by the king of Persia, Ismail I, are the remains of a fortress of the Ourartu period.

Twenty kilometres to the south east of Muradiye, another Ourartu fortress, situated at the place called Körzut Kalesi used to protect the plain of Çaldiran. The rampart of a semi-cyclopian structure was reinforced by projecting towers resembling bastions 10 metres square. In parts the wall is admirably preserved, notably to the south-east where it reaches a height of nearly 8 metres.

We arrive at Lake Van at Bendimahi and join up with the second route—less picturesque but easier—which we will now describe.

We leave Kars by the road we took coming from Erzurum, and we follow as far as Horasan to the place where it meets the well-surfaced highway from Erzurum to Iran which we can follow as far as Doğubayazit if we wish to see this rather extraordinary site, and here we shall find a much better hotel than at Agri. If we do not stay at Agri where there is nothing to see, we take the road which, via Tutak and Patnos, goes towards ERCIS, a little town with about 10,000 inhabitants not far from the north bank of Lake Van.

It has been identified with the former Ardjech of the Arabs

which gave its name to the lake. Ercis was among the possessions of the palatine Davith, lord of Tayq, in 996. In 1055, the town was taken by the Sultan Togril Beg and from that time on, became part of the Seljuk Sultanate of Persia. In the 14th century it fell into the hands of the Kara Koyunlu and became one of their principle centres.

The raising of the level of the lake during the last century has covered up to the south of the modern town the ruins of the ancient city, and we can see appearing here and there towers and mosques, so the only thing worth pointing out is a beautiful *türbe* which we shall see when we reach the borders of the lake; it is the *Hangin Turbesi* of the Mongol period.

Lake Van which is seven times larger than the Lake of Geneva looks just like the sea and has shores of great beauty. In spite of its isolation it could be developed touristically if the Turkish authorities would take the trouble to provide hotels, motels, beaches and suitable roads. Besides the lake itself, buildings and sites would attract visitors if only they were accessible.

It is no good, however, counting on fishing as an attraction; in fact the lake has very few fish, the principle being the darekh, the poor man's herring, on which the neighbouring population feed. We have to admit that sulphur springs 100 metres high on the shores and 200 metres deep in the centre discharge quantities of salt into the water. As we are at 1,780 metres, the temperature is relatively cool even on the sunniest days of summer.

We should add that the level of the lake can vary by as much as three metres and that it is dangerous to venture on it in winter because the storms come very suddenly and without any warning.

The road to Van follows the shores of the lake which here form a sort of headland as far as Bendimahi. We shall see to the right the island of Kadir where the Armenian monastery

of Lim stands and, on the other side of a rocky peak, the ruins
of the castle of Amioux, an Arab enclave of the 8th century
in the kingdom of Vaspourakan.

We pass the Karasu, leaving to the left a promontory at the
end of which is the island of Carpanak with the ruins of the
Armenian monastery of Gdoutz, founded in the 10th century
and restored in the 17th.

We soon arrive at VAN where the modern town is found
separated from the old citadel and from the ancient town which
was abandoned after its destruction in the battles between the
Russians and the Turks in 1917.

Rock inscriptions which we shall find on the hill of the
citadel prove that the origins of Van go back to remote antiquity. From the 11th century B.C. it became the most important
centre of the powerful Ouratu realm which held back the
penetration of the Semites in Asia Minor, more particularly
of the Assyrians. They have brought to light, five kilometres
from the town on a rocky mound called Toprakkale, the
remains of a town which perhaps, under the name of Rusahina,
was the capital of Ourartu after its foundation in the reign
of Rusas I (733–714). After the fall of Nineveh in 621, the
Medes were replaced by the Achaemenian Persians, who occupied the area of Lake Van. The kings of Pontus, who also
claimed Achaemenian origin, succeeded them, and in the
1st century B.C. the region became the centre of the powerful
Armenian kingdom constituted by Tigranes the Great (95–54
B.C.). The country was then under dispute between the Romans
and the Parthians, then the Sassanids. In 643, at the time of
the Arab invasion, Van was occupied by King Theodoros who
shut himself up in his capital on the island of Aghtamar. The
Armenian princes agreed to pay tribute to the Arabs.

In the 11th century came the Seljuk invasion and in the
14th century the domination of the Turcoman dynasty of the
Black Sheep (Kara Koyunlu); in the 16th and 17th centuries
the town was occupied in turn by the Turks and the Persians

and, in 1915, the Russians took over until the armistice of 1917.

The fortress occupies, two kilometres to the west of the modern town, the top of a limestone ridge 1,000 metres long and 100 metres high with the slopes precipitous to the south, but relatively accessible to the north. The highway which follows the escarpment goes near a little oratory surrounded by tombs. We can make out at the foot of the walls the great blocks of the Ourartu fortress, then the Armenian foundation in smaller blocks and, above, the mortar and clay of later periods.

By following round the citadel to the east we find the ruins of the old town of which there remain more particularly two mosques of the Ottoman period with their minarets, their *türbes*, the apse of a church, etc.

Apart from a little archaeological museum where there are Ouratu inscriptions and fragments of sculpture, it is possible to go and see, 5 kilometres away by the road to Özalp, the site of Toprakkale which has already been mentioned. This hill, which is occupied by a military depot, was the residence of King Rusas I (733–714 B.C.), who constructed here a temple dedicated to the god Haldis. Numerous objects in bronze have been discovered and ivory tablets as well as the remains of a temple. An underground staircase cut in a spiral in the rock, comes out at the top of the mound, and leads to a room nearly 50 metres long and 25 metres wide. The cutting of the canal known under the name of Semiran Suyu which used to carry the waters of the river Hoşan to Van, is attributed to King Ouratu Menuas during the 9th century B.C. A few portions of it can be discerned.

We can also go and see, 25 kilometres away to the east, the monasteries of Mt. Varak formerly covered with monastery buildings of which most are now in ruins.

The most important is to be found in the place called Yedikilise. In the 10th century it served as a residence for the

Armenian Patriarch Ananias of Moks I (943–967) and it remained, under Turkish occupation, one of the most important centres of Armenian culture. We can still see there the *Church of the Mother of God* which is preceded by a narthex decorated with paintings of a later date, and the *Church of St. Sophia and St. John* which are not in such a good state of preservation.

We should notice also, to the north in the little valley of Kopanis, the *Monastery of Sourp Grigor* of the 10th century and, near the village of Susans on the western slopes, the *Monastery of Karnivor*.

In the next itinerary we shall see the church of the *Holy Cross of Aghtamar* when we leave Van.

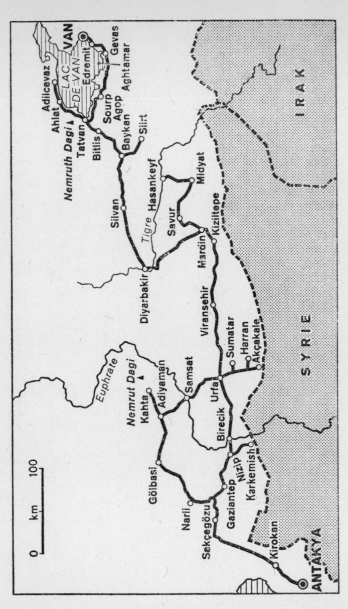

FROM VAN TO ANTAKYA

ITINERARY V

FROM VAN TO ANTAKYA

*Aghtamar — Ahlat — Bitlis — Siirt — Diyarbakir
—Mardin — Midyat — Hasankeyf — Monasteries
of Tur Abdin — Mar Gabriel — Urfa — Sumatar —
Harran — Eski Kahta — Nemrut Daği — Birecik
— Karkemish — Gaziantep — Antakya (Antioch-
on-Orontes)*

THE route follows lake of Van which takes on the most delicate and varied tones according to the time of day. Here there are a whole series of little beaches very popular with the inhabitants of Van on Sundays.

We go through the village of Edremit with its ruined church and, 12 kilometres further on, we see the Şamuran suyu, a broad irrigation canal dating from the Ouratean period and constructed by King Menoua (828–782) to supply his capital with drinking water. Redesigned and restored throughout the centuries, it is still in use. Here and there in the foundations cuniform inscriptions testify to the date it was built and also the dates of the restorations.

The highway crosses the large broad valley of Hosap su and and at the entry to the path which leads to the big village of Gevas we see the *türbe* of Halime Hatun of 1322.

At a wharf in the village of Gevas we shall find, if it has not broken down, the only motor boat which will take us to the islet of AGHTAMAR 5 kilometres from the bank where there

is one of the most magnificent Armenian churches it is possible
to see.

The *Church of The Holy Cross* of Aghtamar, founded by
king of Vaspourakan, Gaguig Ardrouni (904–937), was surrounded by a castle, which has now disappeared and by several
monastic buildings. It was a religious and artistic centre of such
importance that the Bishops of Aghtamar acquired the title of
catholicos which they held until the end of the 19th century
although they had no more than a few hundred parishioners.

The church is designed on a central plan with a dome with,
between the four apses, four niches with corners which enter
into the linking arches of the central dome. It is preceded by
a vast narthex below one of the apses. This is a square divided
into three aisles by four pillars. A porch under an aedicule
surmounted by a pyramid roof has been added later on one
of the other façades. The church may have been built between
915 and 921 by the architect Manuel, and it is considered to
be his masterpiece.

In the interior are rather faded frescoes of the 10th century
which are handled with great skill. The dome rests on a deep
decagonal drum surmounted by a pyramid roof.

But the outstanding interest of the Church of Aghtamar lies
in the carvings which decorate the outside walls and which are
just as remarkable for their decorative quality as for their
modelling. It is extremely rare to see Armenian churches
decorated with figures on the outside. These, which are carried
out in a particularly impressive, monumental style, are applied
at various heights. Above a floral frieze, scenes from the Old
Testament alternate with stylized animals, portraits of
Armenian saints in medallions and animals in high relief, while
higher up, a frieze of foliage links scenes of country life and,
underneath a cornice, are represented masks and animals hunt-
ing each other.

We should take particular notice of the figures of the Evangelists at the four gables. On the west front the *King Gagik*

offering up his church to Christ; on the south front the story of *Noah*, the *Sacrifice of Abraham, David and Goliath*; on the north front, *Adam and Eve*, the *Hebrews in the Furnace, Samson killing the Lion*, and *Daniel in the Den of Lions*.

There are several ruined monastic buildings near the church.

We shall continue to follow the shores of the lake, which we soon leave to penetrate into a mountainous region in order to cross the pass of Satvan 2,350 metres high. A little before we reach this, down below and to the left of the road, we can get to the monastery of SOURP AGOP of the 10th century in a few minutes, whilst to the north on the deserted and precipitous shores of the peninsula of Deve Boynu there still remain some churches founded at the beginning of the 10th century by the king of Vaspourakan, Gagik; *Kamiravank, Sourp Thomas Hin*, etc., but these will only be accessible when a road is completed which will follow the entire shores of the lake.

We go down into the valley of Kümüs where there are several streams which form, in springtime, a lake which slopes down to lake Van by three natural tunnels crossing the northern edge of the rocky hollow on which stand the ruins of the Armenian *Monastery of Sekora*.

We go through Reşadiye and, by means of a little pass before Kotum, we can reach the edge of the volcano of Sekors where the crater is half in the lake.

We arrive at the village of TATVAN on the shores of the lake where the least execrable hotel belongs to the shipping company, Denizcilik Bankasi. Their ships make a tour of the lake either to the south or to the north in eight hours, putting in at Ahlat, Adilocevaz and Ercis to the north, and at Reşadiye to the south.

It is from Tatvan that we can make the ascent of the volcano of Nemrut Daği which should not be confused with its namesake situated on the right bank of the Euphrates; cattle tracks make it possible to reach, in four hours, the edge of the volcano which is a narrow volcanic ledge with a view down into the depths of the crater 500 metres below. There we see a great crescent-shaped lake and the streams of lava in the shape of waves surrounding another smaller lake where the waters are warm.

It is also from Tatvan that, by a little track which crosses several fords, we can get to the village of AHLAT, nowadays practically abandoned, but which enjoyed considerable importance during the middle ages. It lies 32 kilometres away on the edge of the lake.

The town of Ahlat was founded in the 9th century by Kasite Emirs of Malazgirt who used to govern a group of Moslems in Christian territory. Disputed then between the Byzantines, the Georgians and the Marwanide Emirs of Diyabakir it became, in the 12th century the capital of a Moslem state founded by a man called Soukman who took the title of Chah Amen (King of the Armenians) who extended his powers over the entire basin of the Van. The town was occupied by the Mongols in 1245, by the Turcomans of the White Sheep in 1467, but still continued to prosper. Its decadence dates from its capture in 1508 by the Ottomans.

The town was surrounded by walls and dominated by a fortress. On the right bank of the stream we can see the remains of the *Hasan Pasha türbesi* of 1275 and two other mausoleums in ruins, and, after an hour's walk, the troglodyte village of Madarans.

After the ford, the track climbs up to the plateau and crosses a large Moslem cemetery where the numerous *stele* embellished with decorative sculpture often show Armenian influence. To the right there stands a large well-preserved mausoleum; *Ulu Kumbet* of the end of the 13th century which comprises a vast cylindrical funerary chamber with the outer wall decorated with interlacing. Beneath the stalactite cornice runs a white marble band with a Koranic inscription.

To the left on the other side of the track is a whole group of interesting mausoleums: the *Bayndir türbesi* of 1491 is a graceful monument with columns flanking an oratory dating from 1483. We then see anonymous *türbes* of the 18th century, the last two being composed of a square hall covered with a dome on four pendentives, the third on a twelve-sided plan, then the *Iki türbe*, a group of two mausoleums cylindrical on a square base and very well preserved, one of which served as a tomb for the Emir Buğatağaya in 1281 and a second for notables of the city in 1280.

A little further on to the right of the track and below it, the fortress constructed in the reign of Süleyman II in 1554, stands on the edge of the little cliff which overlooks the lake. It was completed by Selim II in 1558. The outer wall, strengthened by round or square towers, is pierced with two gates; the one on the east dates from 1568 inscribed with the name of Selim II and in a citadel where the western rampart, which combines with the *enceinte* of the fortified city, contains the garrison.

Almost opposite the gate of the inner citadel there is a little mosque, *Iskender Pasha Camii*, built by a governor of the town between 1564 and 1570. A second mosque, dating from 1584, can be seen to the east of the wall which links the south east angle of the inner castle to the shores of the lake.

We then go into the new town of Ahlat Ergezen mahallesi and if we continue towards Ercis we shall come to ADILCEVAZ, a township surrounded by huge gardens. It has large walls and a mosque of the Mongol period.

But we only come as far as this, and then turn back to Catvan where we shall take the road to Bitlis.

After 18 kilometres, we pass close to the caravanserai of Bashan of the 13th or 14th centuries, to the left of the road, which, although it is partly ruined, could be converted into a hotel.

Before arriving at Bitlis, we pass two other caravanserais, one of which has been altered into a garage.

BITLIS, which is to be found in the middle of a cool oasis

which contrasts with the arid mountains we have just crossed, is a picturesque and lively little town. It was an Armenian commercial centre in the middle ages and, since the 16th century, the residence of the Kurdish Begs (Lords) who ruled the region of the Van. They did not submit to the authority of the sultanate until 1848.

Beyond the citadel, which dominates the town from the height of its hill and is most attractive with its *enceinte* flanked with polygonal towers, we can see several interesting edifices. To begin with, there is the *Şerefi Camii* of 1528 with its smooth minaret dotted with various decorations. Then the *Medrese Şaraf han* of 1592 built of beautiful golden stone flanked, at the corners, with round towers and with a deep niche decorated with stalactites and framed by graceful sentry boxes; then there are several *türbes* and, in the lower town near the river, a number of mosques, one of which, *Ulu Camii* built in 1126 by the Şerefhans, is now a lively market.

After crossing a pass, we go down into Baykan and, a little further on, we leave, to the left, the road to SIIRT which is only 42 kilometres away and where we can see several monuments, more particularly a number of mosques; the *Ulu Camii* built in 1129 by the Seljuk sultan Mugizzidin Asakir and restored in the 13th century which has nothing left but a minaret, the *Asakir Camii* of the 13th century, and the *Cumhuriyet Camii*, the oldest of the city, which has a lovely door in walnut wood.

The 11th-century baths of Kavvan and the fountain of Sokul Ayn are of the Seljuk period.

Further on we leave to the left a track for GARZAN, 21 kilometres away, and the former Ar zan with its ruined citadel and we shall reach the Batman suyu, a tributary of the Tigris which we cross by a modern bridge next to a magnificent monumental ass-backed bridge which has been very well restored and was built in 1146 on the site of an even older bridge. It is constructed of large dressed blocks and comprises a great pointed arch 35 metres wide and several secondary arches.

We now go through SILVAN, the former Mayafarikin, built on the site of ancient *Martyropolis*. This was founded towards the end of the 4th century by Bishop Marutha who, in 410, gathered together a council at *Seleucis* on the Tigris after which Yezdegerd I, king of the Persians, authorized the celebration of the Christian cult on the territories under his authority. Taken by the Sassanid Persians in 502, it was returned to the Byzantines in 591. It became Arabic in 640 and Turkish at the end of the 11th century.

Only the remains of the ancient ramparts are left and we soon see in the centre of the city the *Ulu Camii*, the Great Mosque, dating from 1227; the prayer hall is covered with a dome on support decorated with rectilinear stalactites.

We continue towards DIYARBAKIR, an important and lively town, lost in a vast arid plain on the right bank of the Tigris. The old town is still surrounded by impressive walls built of black basalt which constitute one of the most splendid specimens of military architecture of the middle ages. It is very much to be regretted that at the moment, when tourism is beginning to penetrate more deeply into these distant regions of Turkey, nothing is being done to preserve them or to put them in order. On the contrary, some strips have been demolished in order to help the circulation of traffic, and some modern buildings have been set up close by. There is no road to enable us to make a complete tour of the exterior which is certainly a pity.

Known under the name of *Amida*, it was disputed by the Parthians, then by the Sassanids and the Romans. In A.D. 115 Trajan, marching on Ctesiphon, seized Southern Mesopotamia from the Parthians. In 297, Galerus, lieutenant of Diocletian, forced the Persians to sign a treaty consenting to the annexing of Nisibe and Amida to the Roman empire. A fortress was built on the artificial mound which dominates the town and, in 349, the Emperor Constantius surrounded the town with ramparts. In 359, seven Roman legions were besieged there by the Persian king, Châphour II (310–379), but the town was retaken by Julian the Apostate during a campaign in Mesopotamia. This latter was killed during his retreat and his successor, Jovian, returned Nisibe to the Persians on condition that the inhabitants should be allowed to withdraw into Roman territory, a circumstance which, in three days, doubled the population of Amida.

As well as this, it was necessary to raise up a new rampart to protect the quarter which had to be laid out beyond the city. To ward off the Sassanid danger, the walls were constantly repaired during the Byzantine period, more particularly in the 6th century in the reign of Justinian. Amida was taken by the Arabs in 638. The Marwanides, at the end of the 10th century, again reinforced the walls. In the middle of the 13th century, the city fell into the hands of the Mongols, then of Tamberlaine and was occupied towards 1515 by the Turks.

We shall first look at the rampart, beginning our tour from the *Harput Gate* still called in the middle ages *Bâb el Armen*, the Armenian Gate or the gate of the Deliverance. It stands on the site of a former gate of the Roman city, later remodelled. This gate, which is very well preserved, opens between two projecting semi-circular towers extended by two perpendicular walls to the ramparts. A machicolated brattice surmounts the gate and to the left a niche of antique origin is opposite another niche of Islamic origin : this latter is decorated with bas-reliefs representing, among other motifs, a bird with outstretched wings and two rampant lions probably dating from 910, the reign of Calif Muktadir. The gate itself is framed by two Byzantine pilasters with capitals decorated with acanthus, supporting an arch which is also of Byzantine origin. On the top of the left tower an inscription, re-used later in the masonry, attributes the construction by Deacon Appius in the 5th or 6th century of a Xenodocheion (Hostelry) which must

17. TREBIZOND : CHURCH OF ST. SOPHIA

20. ANI : CHURCH OF ST. GREGORY OF TIGRANE HONENTZ

have been in the locality of the gate. We find several other inscriptions which have also been re-used; in particular a text engraved in Greek relating the welcome received at Amidir by an envoy of Justinian's and a Latin text mentioning the names of the emperors Gratian, Valens and Valentinian.

Once through the gates, we enter a vaulted passage framed by two barrel vaulted rooms. They used to lead under a portico which in 1056 was surmounted by a mosque with three *iwâns* and which was reached by means of the western tower. The towers comprised two floors and a crenellated terrace.

From the Harput Gate we go on to the *Urfa Gate*. The first five towers of the curtain wall which united them were destroyed in 1931. The curtain wall which still remains measures about 4·50 metres and is reinforced by polygonal towers or half cylindrical ones spaced at intervals of 50 metres. Between two towers the curtain wall is buttressed on the exterior by a jutting bastion two metres wide. At the foot of the rampart is a blind breech protected by a second lower wall which has now disappeared.

On the ninth tower, a badly effaced Seljuk bas-relief represents a sphinx, and an inscription confirms that it was restored in 1237. On the following tower another Seljuk bas-relief, just as effaced, represents a figure holding a hatchet. A postern gate used to open onto the blind breach just before the 13th tower restored in 1091 under the Marwanides. The adjoining bastion was entirely reconstructed in 1163 as is stated by an inscription.

Beyond the site of a postern gate protected by the 16th tower, we reach the Urfa gate which was called *Bab er Roum* in the Middle Ages. This gate originally comprised three passages of which two were probably bricked up under the reign of Ortokide Mohammed in 1183. It opened between two flanking towers about 35 metres apart. Above the gate the keystone of the arch is decorated with a relief of an eagle with outstretched wings above the head of a bull. Two dragons in relief frame the inscription above the gate.

The two iron doors swinging in the basalt sockets probably date from the 12th century, from the Ortokid period. Once we have passed through the gate, we enter a vestibule flanked with guard rooms. The two towers contain a circular room lighted by five loopholes on the ground floor. We can reach the battlemented terrace by the parapet walk, itself reached by stairways constructed parallel to the curtain wall.

The first strip of the curtain wall towards the *Mardin gate*, is of the same type as before; it is reinforced by four towers identical to the preceding ones, and it is pierced with a postern placed under the protection of the third tower. After the fourth tower, the curtain takes a bend to go round a little gulley, the boundaries of which serve as a charnel house and a dump.

The rampart at the bottom of the gulley, was placed beneath two great protective bastions and stronger towers than the rest. As the gulley facilitated surprise sorties, there were three posterns within the space of 60 metres. Beyond the bend the curtain juts out as a salient forming a very sharp angle ending in a powerful circular bastion called Ulu Badan.

The bastion *Ulu Badan* which is isolated from its upper portion is no more than 25 metres in diameter. It is of Byzantine origin, and may have been restored during the Islamic period by the construction of a facing around the base of the tower, then by covering this facing with a mass of masonry so as to form a thick base.

Beyond again, the curtain is reinforced by well-spaced rectangular towers and by buttresses. We reach the Hidden Gate which used to link the citadel with the right bank of the Tigris. Beyond this, the towers are stronger and closer together as in the curtain which links the Urfa Gate with the Harput Gate.

From the Harput Gate we take the Izzet Pasha Caddesi which leads in a straight line to the Mardin gate which may well have been the *Cardo Maximus* of the ancient city, whilst another avenue, also quite straight and perpendicular to it, is doubtless the other *cardo*.

We go past the *Peygamber Camii*, the mosque of the Prophet, built in 1524 in the reign of Süleyman and we then reach the citadel, founded in the 4th century on an artificial mound. It is separated from the town by a curtain wall reinforced with towers which are mainly half-cylindrical. Three gates communicate with the town and a fourth with the exterior.

The two towers defending the principle entrance in the middle of the west front were constructed, like the other bastion of this curtain wall, in the Islamic period on bases of Byzantine towers.

To the south of the redoubt, the Mosque of the Fortress dates from 1160 but has been restored and altered several times.

If we continue to follow the Pasha Caddesi, the most lively street of the city, we shall arrive at a large square which is always very crowded, on to which faces, on one side, the *Hasan pasha Hani* built by the Grand Vizier, Hasan Pasha in 1575; its courtyard is lined with porticoes and has a little fountain. On the other side, stands the *Ulu Camii*, the Great Mosque, the most interesting monument of the town.

According to tradition, it may have been built on the site of a Byzantine church in the style of a Syrian sanctuary.

The large courtyard which we enter has two ablutions fountains and two façades formed by an eastern and western wing. They are of more interest for the originality of architecture than for the numerous fragments of ancient stones which have been used in their restoration. Each wing has a gallery with engaged antique columns surmounted by an upper floor of rooms and nine rectangular bays with lintels surmounted by relieving arches. The antique columns on the ground floor have several drums, but the columns are monolithic on the first floor and crowned with Corinthian capitals. The entrance to the courtyard opens in the central bay which is wider than the others and has a flattened arch. A band of inscription in square Cufic characters runs below the entableture of each storey. The prayer hall is to the left. It has one central nave with a *mihrab* at the back and, on each side, two sections of buildings with three transversal aisles separated by two rows of six pillars of which one is engaged. A long inscription which includes the name of the Seljuk Sultan, Malek Sah, and the date 1091 appears in the frieze on the façade facing the courtyard.

On the other side of the courtyard stands a little oratory and the *Masudiye Medrese* preceded by a portico. The oratory has three aisles separated by two rows of five columns with a little mihrab at the back of the central aisle. The adjoining Masudiye Medrese constructed in basalt, like most of the monuments of Diyarbakir, has a square courtyard dominated by an *iwân* and surrounded on the other three façades with porticoes with arches decorated with festoons or with stepped mouldings.

On leaving the courtyard of Ulu Camii by a gate cut in the west wing, we come out into a lane at the end of which we turn first to the left, then to the right, in order to reach the *Zincirli Medrese* which now houses an archeological museum.

This *Medrese*, which dates from the end of the 1st century, comprises, in keeping with the plan of the Seljuk Koranic schools, a central courtyard with, to the south, an *iwân* flanked by long rooms and, on the other side, rooms for students.

The lanes of this quarter are most picturesque with their houses with overhanging upper storeys and the porches in front of the doors.

Other mosques have a certain interest, in particular the *Behram Pasha Camii* built in 1572, the largest mosque of the town, which is entered by a double portico of nine bays with, in the middle, an entrance with a stalactite arch. In the courtyard the fountain is surrounded by little clustered columns and the *mihrab* in the prayer hall also has a stalactite arch.

We should then take a look at the *Mosque of Nebi*, or of *The Prophet*, which dates from the 15th century and has an entrance flanked with two pink marble columns in a façade which, like the minaret, has alternate rows of black and white stones. The *Kasim Bey Camii* was founded in 1512. It has a minaret flanked with four columns at the base. The *Fatih Pasha Camii* was founded in 1522 by the conqueror of Diyarbakir, Biyirkli Mehmet, whose *türbe* can be seen nearby; the *Husrev Pasha Camii* has a minaret in the Seljuk style with a balcony with stalactites; the *Melik Ahmet Pasha Camii*, built in 1591, has a *mihrab* covered with beautiful glazed tiles like those on the base of the minaret reached by means of two spiral staircases.

There are several churches which were built before the Islamic conquest, of which one is transformed into a mosque and preceded by a large portico with three bays. Behind these rises a façade with three bays in tiercepoint, whilst on the side, a door is surmounted by a trefoil arch. The interior has three aisles.

Another church, *St. George's*, is a prison and cannot be visited. We should mention the churches of *Mar-Stephen*, of *Mor-Zuloro*, of *The Forty Martyrs*, etc., all of which are very little known to tourists.

It should be noted that Diyarbakir is a town where a foreign woman cannot go out alone.

We now turn our steps towards Mardin and, on going out by the gate of that name, we can see, two kilometres away, a bridge across the Tigris of antique origin constructed in 512 by the Metropolitan John Slara who was also responsible for the church of the Forty Martyrs. Built in large, carefully dressed blocks of basalt, it comprises ten unequal arches resting on pylons with projecting sections. Six bands of white limestone bear an inscription of 1065.

The road to Mardin is excellent. After having crossed the plain which surrounds Diyarbakir, we enter a mountainous

region and we soon arrive at MARDIN which is at an altitude
of 1,300 metres on the southern slope of a hill crowned with
the ruins of a citadel built in the 15th century on the remains
of a Roman castro. This latter was known in antiquity by the
name of *Marida*. The city fell into the hands of the Marwanides
at the end of the 10th century and then, a century later, into
those of the Seljuks who returned it shortly afterwards to the
Ortokid Turks who kept their autonomy until 1260. The
citadel resisted the onslaughts of Saladin in 1183 and of one
of his successors in 1198 as well as the Mongols in 1259, but
it was occupied in 1394 by Tamerlaine and conquered in
1431 by the Ay Koyunlu. When the Safavid King of Iran,
Sah Ismail, seized it in 1508 it was, according to the eyewitness
account of a Venetian merchant, populated with more
Christians and Jews than with Moslems. From 1832 to 1840
it was the theatre of a Kurdish revolt.

Since that time Mardin has lost its Catholic Armenian
population and there only remain a few Jacobite and Syrian
Christians.

The houses, built of white limestone, contrast with those of
Diyabakir, the Black. They usually have one storey which leads
on to a covered terrace with two or three arches following
a prototype which goes back to the Middle Ages.

On entering the city we see, to the left on a height, the ruins
of a bastion which used to strengthen the walls of the city and
was linked up to the ramparts of the citadel. We then leave,
on the right, the road to the *Kasim Pasha Medresesi*, built at
the end of the 15th century by Sultan Ak Koyunlu. It is an
impressive building which is reached by means of a stairway.
We enter a vestibule which leads, to the left, to a domed
mosque and, to the right, to a lower court surrounded by porticos except to the north where there is an *iwân*. Two stairways
lead to the two galleries surrounded with cells on the first
storey.

In the main street which crosses the town from east to west,

we find, on the right, the *Latifiye Camii*, built in 1371, which
has an interesting entrance with an alcove with a stalactite arch and a trefoil vault, all surrounded with
arabesques.

A little further on, beyond the Republic Square, a lane leads
to the *Ulu Camii*, bounded to the north by a large quadrangular
courtyard which was surrounded by porticos, but only a few
bays remain. The prayer hall has three aisles separated by two
rows of six pillars. The *mihrab*, which is off axis, is covered
with a cupola. The mosque was founded in the 11th century
and this lack of symmetry is the result of an enlargement of the
14th or 15th centuries. The explosion of a mine during the
Kurdish insurrection of 1832 necessitated works of reconstruction which altered the character of the building.

It is not far from the Cumhuriyet Meydani that we find
the *Sultan Isa Medresesi* constructed in 1385. Steps reducing
the steepness of the ground enable us to reach to the south
a richly decorated portal which gives onto a vestibule. From
here a corridor leads to a prayer hall roofed with a dome on
pillars flanked with two barrel-vaulted halls. At the end of the
corridor, a door leads into the lower courtyard bounded by a
portico and an *iwân* framed by two rib-vaulted halls supported
by a central pillar. On the first floor we come to a terrace and
several rooms; the second terraced interior court with a portico
with depressed arches is over some shops.

From here we can get to the citadel which we enter through
a door with a depressed arch defended by battlements and
surmounted by two passant lions in high relief and an inscription which dates from the Ay Koyunlu and therefore is 15th
century.

By means of a sloping gallery cut into the rock we reach the
summit of the citadel which is on a narrow plateau where there
are some ruined buildings, among them, a mosque with a
square-domed hall and a hall with three aisles which are barrel-
vaulted.

There used to be another mosque at the end of the plateau which dated from the 15th century. Since the plateau is surrounded by steep cliffs, the flanking towers were not very numerous and there remains little of the citadel except a bastion of the 15th century. A residential quarter was situated to the west, and the inhabitants of the lower town found refuge there in times of danger. Since the sides of the hill were vertical in this part, the walls of the houses on the edge of the plateau were sufficient obstacles to ward off assailants.

If we return to the principle street we can see the *Reyhaniye Camii*, then the over-restored *Sehidiye Camii* and finally the *Babusor Camii* of the 14th century.

The principle attraction of the Mardin region lies not so much in the monuments of the town as in following the road that we can see beyond it. This road goes towards Cizre and the Irak frontier.

It is at the 48th kilometre that we shall find, to the right, the road which leads to Savur, a little town situated on a vast plateau known as the TUR ABDIN and considered as the Mt. Athos of the Syrian religion. It was in effect, from the end of the 4th century until the Arab conquest, an active religious centre with numerous monasteries of which several were still occupied by monks at the beginning of the 20th century.

We then go to Midyat where we shall find the ruins of an ancient church, *Mar Philoxenos*, and from which we can reach HASANKEYF, 48 kilometres away on the banks of the Tigris. This little town stands on the site of ancient *Cephe*, a fortification constructed by the Romans at the outlet of the valley of the Tigris on the frontier between the Roman Empire and Persia. Also known as *Cepha* or *Kiphas* in the Byzantine period, it became the seat of an Archbishopric. Towards 640 it was occupied by the Arabs. Vestiges of the great bridge across the Tigris can still be seen and, at the top of the citadel reached through three gateways, the remains of a palace of the

12th century can be distinguished. In the lower town there are several much ruined mosques.

It is also from Midyat, by first taking the road to Hasankeyf but forking off to the right after 7 kilometres, that we can visit several churches belonging to the monasteries of Tur Abdin.

The first, *Mar Yakub*, about 15 kilometres away from Midyat, dates from the 14th century and comprises a vaulted narthex, a single nave also vaulted and planned transversally, and a tripartite sanctuary. It was part of a monastery probably founded from the beginning of the 4th century and which was one of the most important of Tur Abdin. We should notice the carved decoration of the lintel and the jambs of the door which link the narthex with the nave. The entrance to the central Choir is finely carved. The pillars, on which the semi-circular arches rest, are decorated with birds and garlands. The southern façade has a beautiful moulding with carefully dressed stones.

Further on, on the road to Kerburan, at about 20 kilometres from Midyat, we can see *Mar Kyriakos*, the church at Arnas which used to be part of a monastery and which faced a courtyard surrounded with galleries. The cloister of the Choir is 8th-century but the church is older, with the exception of the narthex wall which was rebuilt in the 19th century. The arch of the apse is also carved with distinction.

Not far from Arnas, the church of *Mar Azaziek* of Kefr Zeh is built on the same plan and the choir ends in an apse and is separated from the nave by an iconostatis with four little columns with capitals decorated with acanthus leaves supporting an architrave. The western façade has three windows with pretty mouldings.

To the south of Keyrburan at the end of the track, the village of Kakh has two churches : *Mar Sovo*, now ruined and, more important, *El Hadra*, a graceful little church with a dome decorated on the outside with elegant arcades supported by twin columns with Corinthian capitals. The curve of the dome was formerly covered with a pyramid roof resting on a square base.

A very much restored porch on the site of an older gateway leads into a vaulted narthex flanked by two apses. A door with jambs and a lintel decorated with palm leaves, garlands, pearls and acanthus links the narthex with the nave which is arranged transversally as in several other churches of the Tur Abdin. The dome which rises up over the central crossing is framed by two half domes. The choir has three apses.

We should admire the beautiful decorations of the arches which support the dome and those which link the square to the octagon.

We return to Midyat and 20 kilometres further on, 5 kilometres from the village of Kartmen, we can visit the most interesting monastery of the region of the Tur Abdin, MAR GABRIEL, the Monastery of Kartmen (Quartamin), founded at the beginning of the 5th century by Simeon who succeeded Samuel, a son of an aristocratic family of Mardin who was the real originator of monastic life on the plateau. Under the rule of the Abbot Simeon the monastery became the most important one of the Tur Abdin and housed 400 monks. In 444 the Emperor Anastasius became interested in the monastery which was enlarged; its church was completed in 512 thanks to an imperial subsidy and to workmen and architects sent from Constantinople.

A single door leads to the monastery. We reach the atrium bounded to the east by a gallery which probably formed one side of a cloister and which now constitutes the narthex of the church, Mar Gabriel, the one which was patronized by the Emperor Anastasius. From the narthex we come into the nave which is vaulted and very dark. It is planned transversally, and three low arches open onto the tripartite choir. We can still see on the calotte of the central apse a mosaic cross on a gold background. The left apse gives access to three funerary chambers.

We then go back to the atrium where we shall find an octagonal room with eight radiating niches covered with a dome, and a passage which leads to a long vaulted room which serves as a kitchen and a little courtyard with, at the back, a vaulted arcade leading into the *Church of the Virgin* (el Hadra), now rather broken down, and formed by a *naos* with an inscribed cross, without a dome, and a tripartite sanctuary.

A stairway from this little courtyard leads to the *Church of the Forty Martyrs* doubtless contemporary with the preceding church, but later than Mar Gabriel.

These various sanctuaries are surrounded with the ruins of monastic buildings with, to the west, a church founded in the 4th century in honour of Mar Shim'un and the Mausoleum of Egyptian monks built on an octagonal plan with eight radiating niches each containing a tomb. The octagon is roofed with a very flat dome.

We go back to Mardin and then continue on our way to Urfa. The road goes through Kizeltepe, a large village near which we can see, on the site of the former Koc Hisar, or Dunaysir, an important caravan city of the 13th century and the ruins of a mosque founded in 1200.

We then come to VIRANSEHIR, the ruined town identified as ancient *Constantina* near which we can see the remains of a square *enceinte* from 500 to 600 metres each side, built in basalt and strengthened with round or square towers. It appears to have been built during the Roman period and repaired in the 6th century under Justinian. It was pierced with four entrances, each opening between two semi-circular towers in the centre of each side.

We continue across an arid and monotonous steppe and we again see camels wandering about which we did not see throughout the itineraries along the frontiers of the USSR, of Iran and Irak. We rejoin the road which leads directly to Diyarbakir and come to URFA, a town which is rapidly becoming modernized to the detriment of its old quarters. I have seen there, reduced to a shell and already half demolished, 20 ancient houses built of stone with windows and doors gracefully carved and apparently dating from the 15th century. All this was done to broaden a commercial road when there were plenty of other solutions to be found.

Urfa was, from the first half of the 2nd millennium before our era, the capital of an important state dominated by an Aryan caste opposed to the Egyptian influence. It was named *Hurri* (Grotto) because of the numerous grottoes in the neighbouring mountain chain of Nemrut Daği. This Hurrite state formed with the neighbouring state of Mitanni the nation known as Hanigalbat. It represented one of the aspects of that great migration of peoples lead by the Kassites in Mesopotamia. They replaced the Babylonian and Elamite dynasties whilst the Hyksos invaded Egypt and dominated it for a century and a half. This Aryan aristocracy, skilled in training horses which they employed in wheeled war chariots, enabled the Hurrite people to impose their rule in northern Mesopotamia, in Syria and in Asai Minor. The two states which were intermingled with Egypt were destroyed towards 1370 B.C. by the Hittite king Suppiluliuma.

With the arrival of Alexander the Great, the population was mainly based on Aramaic people who called the town Orhai. It was to be called *Edessa* by the Macedonians before becoming, towards 132 B.C., the capital of an Emirate which kept its autonomy for four centuries.

This principality of the Abgar together with the Israelite nation, led the Semitic reaction against the Hellenism imposed by the kings of Antioch. By converting them to Christianity towards 204, Abgar IX favoured the cultivation of Syriac literature which contributed to the development of the Arab civilization.

The province of Urfa was the setting for wars in which the Romans fought against their enemies beyond the Euphrates and more particularly the defeat of Crassus in 53

B.C. and of Valerian in 260. In the 4th century we see St. Ephram installed at Urfa and founding a school of Theology known as the School of the Persians, where the Nestorian conclusions were at variance with the Basilei who, from 457, banished the Doctors from Edessa and in 439 closed down the school. Captured by the Sassanids in 605 and recaptured by Heraclius, it was occupied by the Arabs in 637, then bought back by the Byzantines who kept it until 1087. It was then that the arrival of the Crusaders turned it into a Latin principality for 50 years. All these battles which we briefly describe, are doubtless the reason why there are so few interesting remains of the past of the city of Urfa.

We see, on the hill dominating the town, the remains of the citadel built by the Crusaders. It is protected on two sides by a broad deep ditch cut in the rock and, as well as several sections of curtain wall reinforced by towers, we can see vestiges of antique constructions among which two columns, with one with an inscription in Syriac, is known as the Throne of Nimrod. They are crowned still with Corinthian columns.

At the foot of the citadel flows the ancient spring of Rohas, or the fountain of Callirhoe, where the waters form a great pond full of enormous carp which leap out when you offer them food. The inhabitants consider them sacred and they will assure you that Abraham stopped here at the time of his wanderings which lead him from Ur to the land of Canaan. This stretch of water is to be found in a large public park intersected with fish ponds bordered with several attractive buildings and a mosque which is much restored.

On theother side of the square, the *Abder Raman Medresesi* of the 17th century has a courtyard surrounded by cells for Koranic Theological students and a little mosque.

If Urfa is of limited interest, it is, all the same, a point of departure for several excursions which we will mention.

We can, for instance, first take to the south the road to Akçakale on the Syrian frontier to see Sumatar and Harran.

After 18 kilometres we shall find a track to the left for SUMATAR, where we can see a strange pagan sanctuary consecrated by the Sabians to the seven planets and to their Supreme god.

Let us say a few words about the religion of the Sabians who had originally worshipped from the most remote antiquity the lunar god Sin whose principle sanctuary is to be found at Harran or nearby. The Sabians venerated a supreme divinity described as Sumatar under the name of Marihala. His cult symbol was a pillar and he governed the universe by the intermediary of the divinities of the planets : Helios, the god of the sun, Sin, the god of the moon, Cronos, Saturn, Bel, Jupiter, Ares, Mars, Balti, Venus and Nabuq and Mercury. Every day of the week was dedicated to a planet and the Sabians observed certain numbers of fasts; the one consecrated to the god of the moon lasted for 30 days. Their cult was made up of a curious mixture of various philosophies, more particularly Neoplatonic and of Babylonian astronomy. These cults also comprised ritual sacrifices and mysteries with initiation rites. The movements of the sun governed the rhythm of the prayers, and invocations were addressed to the gods at dawn, at midday and at sunset.

The Sabian cult was practised at Harran after the adoption of Christianity by the kings of Orhai-Urfa and even after the Arab conquest, at least until the 12th century and perhaps until the 17th. This was with Judaism and Christianity one of the three religions tolerated by Islam, even though the habits of the Sabians at times shocked the Moslems, as for instance their clothes and their long hair.

The sanctuary of Sumatar also comprises the remains of seven buildings arranged in a circle around a central mound or sacred hill. They are probably miniature temples dedicated to the planets. Six of them have an underground crypt with one or several chambers and one entrance orientated towards the sacred hill.

This latter is surmounted by two rupestral bas-reliefs one of
which is a man with a halo standing in a niche with a carved
archivolt. A Syriac inscription states that it dates from 164
A.D. The other carving is a bust in a niche with inscriptions.
Nine other Syriac inscriptions are carved on the face of the
rock.

On another mound about 500 metres away a cubic building
is a temple of the sun god. It is composed of a single hypethral
chamber—that is to say open to the sky, the side wall about
2 metres long with, on three sides, *arcosolia* surmounted by
projecting arches. A kilometre away from the central mound,
also to the west, rises up on a tumulus a circular stone construction with its outside wall strengthened by eight pilasters. A
ramp enables us to descend into a crypt with two chambers
linked by a narrow passage with in each of them two *arcosolia*.
It may have been consecrated to Saturn.

A second circular building, which is now reduced to its
foundations, is to be found a kilometre away and may have
been consecrated to Jupiter, whilst a third, more to the north,
may have been dedicated to Saturn and a fourth to Venus.

Two others may also have had a sacred function, the first
being dedicated to Mercury and the second to Mars. The latter
is composed of a series of pillars standing near a headless statue
of a man resting his hand upon the hilt of his sword. A courtyard hewn out of the rock is to be found near the police station.
We should also notice some medieval remains on the hill to
the north and, about 600 metres from the mound, a double
grotto with bas-reliefs and Syriac inscriptions. In the first, two
figures carved in relief represent the *toparch* Wael and his
son and, on the far wall the larger-than-life effigy of a man
carved by order of Bar Nahar in honour of Aurelius Hafsai, the
slave freed by Antonius Caesar. More to the right an empty
niche is flanked by emblems of the moon god and, right at the
end, another figure in relief of the same Hafsai. On the other
side, wall traces may still be distinguished of another carving,

Tiridates, son of Adona, then three rough sculptures depicting a son of Adona, the *toparch* Agbar and the *toparch* Bar Bahar and a relief representing a child. Some of these bas-reliefs and inscriptions date from A.D. 164 and others from between A.D. 150 and 200.

We return to the road to Akcakale and, 13 kilometres further on, we find a track which leads to HARRAN 11 kilometres away.

This little village with curious houses in the shape of anthills like those in the north of Syria, occupies the site of ancient *Carrhes*, an important fortress mentioned in Genesis under the name of Charan. Abraham may have lived here for several years during his journeying. Harran is also mentioned in a text from Mari recorded about 2000 B.C. on the subject of a treaty which may have been signed in the Temple of Sin. This was restored at least three times by Samanazar III (859–824) and by Assurbanipal and Nabonidus in 553. During the wars between the Romans, the Parthians and the Sassanids, the fortress of Carrhes became an important base. In 217 Caracalla, returning from the Temple of Sin to his palace, was assassinated there by Macrinus.

During the Byzantine era, the emperor Theodosius had the Temple of Sin destroyed in 382 and, in the 6th century, Justinian rebuilt the ramparts. The Arabs seized it in 639 and they respected the rights of the two sections of the city, Christian and Sabian. In the Ommayad period, Harran was the favourite residence of Marwan II. In 1104, the Crusaders were repelled; in 1149, Nur ed Din seized it and, in 1260, the Mongols destroyed it.

Harran was surrounded by an *enceinte* which is now ruined but can still be distinguished as well as the seven gates which led into the town. Near a hamlet close to two ruined bastions is the mosque and the tomb of Sheik Ayat el Harrani. We then come to the Aleppo Gate which is quite well preserved and which was restored by Saladin in 1192. Further on we reach

21. ANI : CHURCH OF ST. GREGORY OF ABOUGHAMRENTZ

22. VAN : THE CITADEL

23. AGHTAMAR

24. BITLIS : SARAF HAN

the site of the Raqqa Gate and the citadel which occupies the site of the temple of the Sabian god of the moon, transformed into a fortress in 1032. It comprises an irregular *enceinte* reinforced at the corners by polygonal towers of which three are still standing. In the interior stands an imposing edifice of three storeys. Originally the fortress was independent of the *enceinte* of the town and surrounded by a moat. The castle was restored several times, more particularly in 1098, a little before the Frankish conquest, then by the Franks towards the end of the occupation of Harran.

We then turn our steps towards the Great Mosque with its tall minaret; we shall find it near an artificial hill which occupies the site of the primitive city.

The Great Mosque founded by Marwan II (744–750) was enlarged after the Calif El Ma'mun passed through in 830 and then restored by Saladin. In the ruins are three *stele* connected with King Nabonidus who reigned in the first half of the 6th century.

To the west, we can see the ruins of a building with an apse not far from the Mosul Gate. As we go towards the Lion Gate we come across the vestiges of a mosque, then of a church with three aisles, the central one ending in an apse.

We return to Urfa from which we can reach—admittedly with very great difficulty—the tomb of Antiochus I on the Nemrut Daği. This excursion is an adventure since the road is extremely bad and it is scarcely possible without the help of a jeep and a journey on foot.

We leave Urfa by the road to Diyarbakir and, after 11 kilometres, we take to the left the one which leads to Adiyaman. It is particularly bad between Bozova and Samsat.

ADIYAMAN, founded in the 7th century under the name of *Hisn Mansur*, still has the remains of an Arab castle restored by the Seljuks, and the *enceinte* of the city with three gates.

SAMSAT, ancient *Samosata*, on the right bank of the Euphrates, was important from Roman times. It is the birthplace of the writer Lucian who was born there at the beginning of the 2nd century, and of St. Lucian (235–312) who was martyred at Antioch. Taken and retaken by the Byzantines and the Arabs it was occupied by the Crusaders and, at the end of the Middle Ages, it rapidly declined.

We take the road twords Kâhta from which we reach Eski Kâhta, the point of departure for Nemrut Daği. It is possible to hire mules and a guide there by asking the village mukhtar.

Ten kilometres further on, we pass along the foot of the hill of Karakus where stands a Roman column supporting a double-headed eagle, the second head having been worn away by the passage of years. Then we pass by an old Roman bridge across the Cendere Suyu and reach the medieval fortress of Yeni Kale which is on a hill overlooking the right bank of the ancient Nymphaeus and which is quite well preserved. We should notice particularly a fortified way constructed in a fissure of rock which enabled defenders to reach the river.

A track to the right crosses the Kâhta Cayi over an old Seljuk bridge at the entrance to some impressive gorges.

We soon come to ESKI KÂHTA, a little village situated near the ruins of ancient *Arsameia ad Nymphaeum*. Here excavations have unearthed interesting remains of a funerary sanctuary constructed by Antiochus I of Commagenes for his father Mithradates.

After crossing the Nymphaeum across a Seljuk arched ass-backed bridge, we take a little path which leads first of all to a platform cut into the rock where there used to be two *stele* just before the antique supporting wall of a terrace at the end of which there was an antechamber cut into the rock and a little fountain. From there we can reach a huge rupestral chamber by means of a stairway cut in the rock. We then arrive at another terrace where there was another stele near an important rupestral inscription in Greek characters on five columns, and a relief figuring Heracles welcoming a king of Commagenes, probably Mithradates.

On the little plateau which extends over the summit of the hill of Eski Kale, there used to be several edifices, one with a mosaic floor. Down below, a rupestral inscription decorates a platform which was originally linked to the hierothesion of Mithridates by a stairway cut into the rock. Grooves were used for the setting up of two stele decorated with reliefs, one of which represents the god Mithra with a Phrygian cap.

Those who have driven to Eski Kâhta in a jeep, can hire mules at this point and a guide to take them to the summit of NEMRUT DAĞI where Antiochus I erected his colossal hierothesion. It is a three to five hours walk to this extraordinary monument which the King consecrated to his own cult, to his ancestors and to Greco-Persian divinities. It was during excavations carried out from 1953 onwards that this gigantic sanctuary was discovered. It is composed of a 150-metres high tumulus of three terraces. Those on the east and the west comprise a central court surrounded by huge statues eight to ten metres high, of lions, of daises etc., in which Hellenistic and Anatolian traditional styles are mixed with Hittite characteristics. On the east terrace a double platform which used to extend in front of the statues had notches or slots into which was fitted an aedicule in the form of a baldaquin decorated with reliefs of Antiochus of Commagenus welcomed by the gods, and his lion horoscope.

During the passage of years this grandiose dream remained forgotten by men and became the target of erosion, lightning and earthquakes. The terraces were torn away, the statues decapitated. Archaeologists have found enormous heads and have arranged them around the extraordinary tumulus. Careful search has been made for a funerary chamber or a temple inside the mound, but these excavations, carried out with extreme care have only resulted in falls of earth, and the Pyramid of Antiochus I will probably always withhold its secret, but it remains as a witness to the incredible vanity of the powerful men of this world.

The tiring effort of making this journey is rewarded by the

beauty of the sculpture which decorates the sanctuary and also by the splendour of the mountain landscape to be seen from the height of the terraces of the temple.

We go back to Adiyaman and, instead of returning to Urfa, we continue to Gaziantep by way of Gölbasi and Narli.

Those who did not go to Nemrut Daği should drive through BIRECIK, a little town along the banks of the Euphrates overlooked by the ruins of a fortress perched on a peak of rock. The Crusaders may have been partly responsible for its construction. The curtain wall is strengthened by strong rectangular towers with three storeys of casemates; a slope of masonry protects it from being undermined.

We then continue to Nizip where we take, at the entrance to the town, a road to the left for the village of Barak which is on the Syrian frontier.

Near Barak, in Turkish territory, is the site of KARKEMISH, capital of the most powerful of the Hittite kingdoms which prospered after the collapse of the New Hittite Empire of Anatolia.

Before the invasion of Anatolia by the tribes known as the "People of the Sea", Karkemish was dependent on the Hittite kings of Anatolia as well as being under the influence of the Hurrites.

After the fall of Boğazkale, the kings of Karkemish regained their independence, conceding the disc of the Sun, ancient imperial Hittite emblem, and the title of "Great King" and contented themselves from that time forward with the title of "Lord of the country".

The Hittite principalities had many times to repel attacks of the Assyrian troops, and they had to become tributaries of their powerful neighbour before being eventually annexed in 717 b.c. in the reign of Sargon II.

Excavations have made it possible to trace the three *enceintes* of the town corresponding to successive enlargements and to discover numerous bas-reliefs which used to decorate the gates of the city, as well as several foundations of monuments. These rather rough carvings represent mythological scenes, processions of warriors and of courtiers. They recall Assyrian art but with something rather less hieratic and more human. Most of them have been taken to the Hittite museum in Ankara.

The city used to be composed of two distinct sections : the inner town which was fortified and the outer town.

The inner city was surrounded by a wall which followed the bank of the Euphrates and had one gate. It encircled the citadel situated on a hill 40 metres high which overlooks the banks of the river. Beyond, the rampart was extended to the north by a tower, called the Mill, and a fortress, whilst to the west and to the south the wall separated the inner city from the outer city which it communicated with by two gates.

The Palace stood in the centre of the inner town. Access to it was by a wide, monumental way running between walls.

Finally, 20 kilometres to the north of Nizip, all that remains of an ancient city are strips of walls of the citadel perched on a hill on the shores of the Euphrates as well as fragments of an enormous statue dating from the Roman era.

We return to the road to Urfa and soon reach GAZIANTEP, an important town of modern aspect which has developed in a vast plain between two hills, one of which is crowned with the ruins of a medieval fortress. This artificial hill proves that there already existed a little built up area on this site from the period of Tell Halaf, that is to say, towards 3,800 to 3,500 B.C. but it attained its greatest importance towards the middle of the 2nd millennium and more especially in the course of the 1st millennium, at the time of the Syro-Hittite principalities, of which we met an example at Karkemish. These principalities disappeared at the end of the 7th century B.C. when they were annexed by Sargon II known then under the name of Aïntab. Gaziantep was occupied towards the end of the 11th century by the Seljuks who built a fortress there.

This fortress, constructed on an artificial hill and a rocky spur, is in course of restoration. It is not necessary to climb to the summit, but one of the sites is quite well preserved with a square tower below it and the bastion of the entrance gate defended by a barbican and a deep moat.

In a Seljuk *medrese* they have set up a little archaeological museum to house the Hittite bas-reliefs found at Karkemish, at Sakçegözü and at Zendjirli; seals and cylinders from various periods and objects of folk lore.

We continue towards Antakya, taking to begin with the road to Adana which, 75 kilometres further on, goes near *SAKÇEGÖZÜ* where excavations have laid bare a number of remains super-imposed in twelve layers of debris in an artificial mound called Coba Hoyuk. The earliest occupation dates back to the 5th millennium and the others developed up to the Assyrian period. After a long gap the site was reoccupied in the Middle Ages during Moslem times.

We then fork to the right to KIROKAN a former caravan centre and large township; then we leave, to the right, the track for the castle of Bagras which we shall describe in the next itinerary, and drive along a beautiful road bordered with trees, soon arriving at ANTAKYA which we can call *Antioch-on-the-Orontes*.

This town which is pleasantly situated in the valley of the Orontes between Kizil Dağ and Mount Cassius, is renowned for the mildness of its climate enlivened by a sea breeze even in the height of summer.

It is not of very ancient origin because it was only in 307 B.C. that Antigonus founded upstream from the actual city, a town called *Antigonia*. It was replaced seven years later by another, founded by Seleucus which was called Antioch on a particularly well chosen site. It first developed on the left bank of the Orontes and to this quarter three others were soon added, each with its own wall inside a communal enclosure wall. Very soon the city became covered with monuments, decorated with statues by famous artists. As this town was composed of different ethnic elements it had a troubled existence, especially after the death of a monarch. The political preponderance was held mainly by Greco-Macedonians, and was composed for the most part of Macedonian and Cretan Colonists, while the suburbs were inhabited by natives of Aramaic culture. There was also an important Jewish colony; thus, in the 2nd century B.C. the town which counted 500,000 inhabitants, was just as much a business centre as a city of luxury and pleasure seeking. It was renowned in the Oriental world for its games and its feasts and its cult of Apollo.

Weary of the disagreements in the Seleucid dynasty, the inhabitants appealed to the king of Armenia, Tigranes the Great (95–54 B.C.), who occupied the town in 83 B.C. and gave it 14 years of security to which the Romans put an end, wishing to decide for their own profit the problem of the succession of the Seleucids. In 64 B.C. Pompey seized the region of Antioch which was then declared a Roman province whilst the capital city was declared free. In spite of several earthquakes in the course of which Trajan narrowly escaped death, the town preserved its brilliant activities whether commercial, literary or artistic. There was more especially a school of Philosophy with Theologians who were remotely disciples of Aristotle. The Jewish colony was augmented by numerous Jews exiled from Palestine shortly after the death of Christ. These latter set about converting the pagan population to Christianity. They had for their leaders, St. Barnabas, helped later on by St. Paul. St. Peter sojourned in Antioch for several years and a number of bishops suffered martyrdom there, notably St. Exodus and St. Ignatius, executed in Rome in A.D. 107.

In 260 the town was taken by Châhpour I, king of Persia, who deported part of the population to Susiana.

When Christianity became the official religion, the churches which had been destroyed by Diocletian were reconstructed and the Emperor Constantius himself consecrated a great church there in 341. Antioch regained its spiritual influence and became a training centre for architects who covered the north of Syria with splendid sanctuaries. The Bishop of Antioch was considered to be one of the spiritual chiefs of the Eastern church and it was in A.D. 340 that the bishops of Antioch, of Cesarea and of Constantinople manifested their separatist tendencies in supporting Arianism, a heresy of Oriental origin already condemned in 325 at the Council of Nicaea. It was at a council held in 341 at Antioch that the formula of Arianism was confirmed by which the church marked her independence from the church of Rome.

In 526 the city was entirely destroyed by a violent earthquake which caused 250,000 deaths in the province. In 540 it was captured by Khosroes I who took some of the population to captivity in Mesopotamia.

Justinian, having retaken the town, rebuilt the walls, but Antioch was again occupied by the Arabs who remained there for more than 300 years. It was not in fact until 969 that the Byzantine troops recaptured it, but in 1079 it was under the power of an Armenian adventurer and finally, later on, it was in the hands of the Seljuks. In 1097 it was besieged by the Crusaders who succeeded in capturing it and who made it for 170 years the seat of a Latin principality founded by Bohemond.

Antioch regained prosperity which came to an end in 1268 when it was taken and entirely destroyed by the Sultan Baïbars at the head of his Mameluks of Egypt. Placed under a French mandate at the end of the First World War, it was given back to Turkey in 1939 with the Sandjak of Alexandretta.

We shall see, to begin with, on the road to Samandag, the museum of ceramics which houses a most remarkable collection of mosaics found in the region. Then, on the road to Aleppo, from the other side of the Orontes, we come to *The grotto of St. Peter* which we shall find to the right at the foot of the mountain.

It was here that the early Christians met together. The façade which has been restored, dates from the time of the Crusades. It has three rose windows which light the interior of the grotto where we can see a spring, the remains of a rough mosaic and, to the left, a little redoubt which leads to a narrow tunnel which must have been a means of escape for the faithful if they were taken by surprise.

A hundred metres above the grotto a curious and very much worn relief represents a bust flanked by a standing figure. It may be Antigonus, the lieutenant of Alexander the Great, and his successor in Asia, or of Seleucus I Nicator.

Practically nothing at all remains of the ancient city. The main highway, into which ran the other arteries, used to continue for 4 kilometres north to south. It was flanked with porticoes along its whole length at the beginning of the 2nd century. The fairway made of great slabs of hard limestone was 9·60 metres wide. The porticoes, 10 metres deep, were bordered with shops and had no less than 3,200 columns, many of which were of grey or pink granite. After the earthquakes of 526 and 528, Justinian only rebuilt a part of these porticoes. The centre of the city was marked by a vast circular space from which there went, at right angles, another highway bordered with porticoes linking the Porta Media to one of the bridges across the Orontes. The remains of these highways were found four or five metres beneath the present level of the land. As for the forum of Valens, it was built across the torrent of Parmenios and spanned it with several arches.

The remains of the Byzantine city are just as sparse. We need only point out, near a mosque built in the 19th century, on the site of a church, a little sanctuary which stands above a Byzantine crypt.

The citadel, which crowns the rocky peak of Mt. Silpios, from which there is a magnificent panorama, dates from its later phase, from the time of Nicephoras Phocas, with numerous restorations carried out by Basilus II at the beginning of the 11th century and also by the Crusaders. It occupied the summit of a rock which was very difficult of access and the fortifications comprise a curtain wall linked by two little round towers, while the city was entered by a gate cut in the southern porch. The fortress itself comprised in the interior a vast *enceinte* which was almost intact in 1831. The Egyptians used it as a quarry for the construction of huge barracks and after that the population followed their example.

The sections which are the most difficult to reach are the best preserved. Made up of two faces of dressed stone with, in the centre, a thick section of mortar, the walls go back to the period of Theodosius. They were reinforced by massive towers of three storeys, and the fortified city was five to six times more extensive than modern Antioch.

The surrounding places are no better preserved than Antioch itself. Of *DAPHNE* which lies 9 kilometres away, there only remains the site where the nymph Daphne, followed by Apollo, was changed into a laurel bush. Strict regulations forbad touching these trees and it was in this idyllic setting of laurels, of cypress and of leaping cascades that Seleucus I built a temple to Apollo where the famous statue was the work of Bryaxis. There are several sanctuaries here, of which one, dedicated to Olympian Zeus by Antiochus IV Ephiphanes is enclosed a chriselephantine statue. A deep grotto, reached by several steps, was perhaps dedicated to Hecate.

The richer citizens of Antioch built themselves villas at Daphne which became a city of pleasure famous for its orgies. Pompey had a predilection for Daphne and he enlarged its territories and, later, Titus, with the spoils from the pillage of Jerusalem, constructed a theatre there. In the 3rd century a Christian basilica, built opposite the theatre of Apollo, housed the relic of St. Babylas. The temple was destroyed later on by a fire for which the Christians were held responsible. The churches, restored during the Byzantine period, disappeared under the Arab occupation and of all this brilliant past nothing

remains in this charming site except a few sections of walls
and a few bases of columns.

We can also go to Margaracik, SELEUCIA PIERIA.
Thirty-two kilometres away, this little hamlet stands on a hill
which overlooks a vast beach at the mouth of the Orontes.

Seleucia Pieria was founded in A.D. 300 by Seleucus
Nicator. It was a very prosperous fort, but, the victim of many
earthquakes, it ended up by falling into oblivion.

Nothing remains but insignificant vestiges and the canal cut
in the rock in the reign of Vespasian.

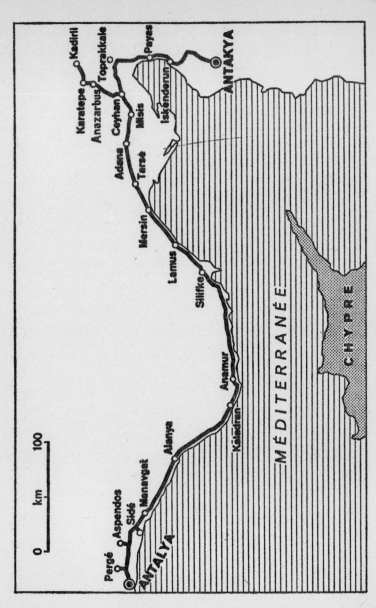

FROM ANTAKYA TO ANTALYA

ITINERARY VI

FROM ANTAKYA TO ANTALYA

Bağras — Iskenderun — Toprakkale — Misis —
Adana — Tarsus — Mersin — Soles — Eloeusa —
Neapolis — Korigos — Kaya — Anamur — Syedra
— Alanya — Sida — Aspendos — Perga — Antalya

THIS Itinerary, which follows the coast all the way, is
planned to include a whole series of ancient towns which
alternate with pretty beaches provided with comfortable
motels where one can bathe and relax. The road is very well
laid out and often high above the sea, providing splendid
panoramas.

A beautiful road lined with trees constructed during the
French occupation goes towards Iskenderun. After driving for
25 kilometres we can take a rather bad track to the left which
covers the 4 kilometres to the castle of BAGRAS (Baghras).
This is ancient *Pagras* mentioned by Strabo. It used to command the highway over the pass of Belen. After the foundation of Antioch on the Orontes it became the advance defence
post of the Seleucid capital.

At the time of the Crusades, the castle was of primary
importance for the protection of the capital of the principality
of Antioch. The Crusaders, who named it Gaston or Gastin,
used it as one of their principal fortresses. Towards the end of
1188 Sultan Saladin captured it, but Leon II, Cilician king
of Armenia, recaptured it and restored it. As he refused to
surrender it to the princes of Antioch, he was threatened with
reprisals by the Crusaders and he finally handed it over to the

Templars. In 1268 it capitulated when besieged by Baïbars.

The fortress is built upon a rocky peak, precipitous, especially on the western side. The castle is approached from the east and on this side there are two *enceintes* dominated by a redoubt composed of a huge rectangular keep constructed of small masonry, a great hall and a chapel. An underground room supported by enormous pillars may have been built by the Crusaders. There are a number of other rooms built of inferior masonry.

An aqueduct, which is quite well preserved, used to carry water to the fortress from several springs in the mountain. Another spring which flows at the foot of the rampart was called the *Fountain of Gastin* in the Middle Ages.

We go on to Cakalli from which we can reach Amik Golu, the Lake of the Depression, which fills the centre of a fertile plain where a number of prehistoric sites have been found.

The road now winds up towards the Pass of Gelen, Pylae Syriae, 644 in altitude, then descends to the picturesque village of Belen and, after a last spur of Kizil Dağ we come to ISKEN-DERUN, formerly Alexandretta, a large port at the head of a gulf surrounded by a fertile plain. This modern town holds no interest for us except for its fish restaurants on the shores of the lake.

The road continues towards Adana a little way in from the coast and leaves to the right PAYAS which has a small mosque of the 16th century, a *bedestan* and an Ottoman fortress then, 27 kilometres further on, the ruins of the *Epiphania* founded during the Seleucid period, with the remains of an aqueduct.

We are in the plain of Issus where the celebrated battle took place in which Alexander the Great was victorious against the King of Persia, Darius III, in 333 B.C.

He had already reached Myriandus when, learning that the Persians were at the rear of the army cutting it off from its bases, he turned about. Darius III had assembled the main part of his cavalry on the right flank, placed his Greek mercenaries in the centre and his light infantry on the left. Alexander confronted the Persian cavalry, commanded by General Naharsanes, with his Thessalian cavalry, placed his heavy Macedonian phalanx in the centre, whilst a corps of archers, reinforced by 300 cavalry chosen from his personal guard, threw back the Persian infantry at the first attack.

After having crossed the river which separated the two armies, the phalanx got into difficulties, so Alexander went to their help, brought up some of his cavalry to support them and, perceiving the Royal chariot, he opened up a passage across the Persian lines. A fearful conflict broke out around Darius' chariot. Fearing capture, the king fled on horseback. On seeing this catastrophe his troops disbanded and the retreat was so sudden that the imperial family and all the baggage of Darius fell into the hands of the Macedonians. This victory opened up the route to Syria for Alexander.

We then proceed on foot to the castle of TOPRAKKALE, built in the 12th century by the Armenians at the outlet of the narrow valley which commands the plain of Issus. It is well preserved with two *enceintes* flanked by round towers.

We come to a fork and, leaving to the right the road for Gaziantep and Maras, we continue towards CEYHAN, a populous town which spreads over the right bank of Ceyhan Nahr and from which we can visit Kadirli and Karatepe which are 61 and 84 kilometres away respectively.

We first go through Aysehoca from which a road to the right takes us to the little village of Anavarza, 4 kilometres away, and situated near the ancient runs of *ANAZARBUS* probably founded after the 1st century B.C. and flourishing during the Roman period. Metropolitan city of Cilicia Secunda under Theodosuis II (408–450), it was destroyed and rebuilt twice at the beginning of the Byzantine era and was successively named *Justinopolis* and *Justinianopolis* in honour of Justin and of Justinian who had contributed to its rebirth. Several times pillaged by the Arabs in the 7th and 8th centuries, it became the Arab town of *Ain Zarba*. The Califs, Haroun-el-Rashid and Mutawkil, raised up the walls again and it was retaken by Nicephorus Phocus in 964; it then fell into the hands of the Armenians and Torus I made it his capital in 1137. It was retaken by the Emperor John Comnenus and the Byzantines kept it until 1144. It became Armenian again until the beginning of the 13th century, and was ravaged again and again by the Mamelukes and ended up by being abandoned after having been taken from the Armenians in 1375.

The lower town used to lie at the foot of the rocky hill crowned with the ruins of the medieval citadel. The acropolis itself was in the centre of it, the highest and narrowest part which was the easiest to defend. To the west, the castle was protected by a steep cliff, whilst, to the east, a difficult climb was preceded by a natural moat made by the bed of the river Sumbas. An *enceinte* also surrounded the lower town; it was built by the Armenians on existing Byzantine foundations.

On arrival we can see a piece of the highway which linked Anazarbus to Misis, the remains of a little bridge which carried it over a stream and, at the foot of the hill, two columns which formed part of an amphitheatre.

Some fragments of the monumental entrance to the Roman stadium still remain and some sarcophagi of the necropolis can be seen on a spur.

By continuing to follow the foot of the hill, we reach the site of the much ruined theatre with, above on the slope of the acropolis, other sarcophagi and two rupestral reliefs representing a scene of the *palaestra* with four athletes and a winged figure on a dolphin.

More to the north, a piece of the *enceinte* of the lower town was reinforced by towers spaced at regular intervals and preceded by a masonry ditch 7·45 metres wide and protected by an outer wall.

By skirting this rampart we reach the triumphal arch, the most interesting monument in Anazarbus. Corinthian in style,

25. DIYARBAKIR : WALLS

28. ALANYA : RED TOWER

it may date from the 3rd century A.D. The central arch reserved
for the passage of vehicles is wider than the two others which
were for pedestrians. A corridor linked the three arches together.
The outer face was decorated with two pairs of Corinthian
columns on each side of the central carriageway and by a
single one between the side arches and the small walls jutting
out at right angles at both extremities. The entablature which
surmounted it merged above the central passage with the arch
of this opening resting on two pillars.

On the city side, the triumphal arch is less well preserved.
It does not seem to have had any columns, but the central
carriageway is framed by two niches three metres high with
a consol decorated with acanthus leaves which presumably
supported a statue.

Then we find vestigial remains of a town gate and approxi-
mately level with the second section of the encircling wall,
the ruins of the so-called South West Church of which only
the foundations remain. If we continue still further, we shall
come upon the ruins of two Byzantine aqueducts, the sparse
remains of Roman theatres and of the *Church of the Holy
Apostles*, perhaps of the 6th century, on a plan of three aisles
with a single apse.

We can climb to the upper town from the theatre by means
of a stairway cut into the rock. It passes near a small Byzantine
oratory, formerly decorated with paintings of which little
remain but the *Head of Christ*.

The fortress was composed of two individual enclosure walls
separated by two moats hollowed out of the rock, and a tower
formerly the redoubt. The first *enceinte* to the south may have
been established during the Byzantine period, but the
Armenians rebuilt the south wall and repaired the gate in the
centre of the east wall. It still encloses the funerary church
of the Cilician Armenian kings at the time when Anazarbus
was their capital. It is a church with three aisles each terminating in an apse. The only remaining paintings which decorate it

M

are *Christ Pantocrator*, on the central apse, represented upon a throne surrounded by seraphim and, in medallions, portraits of four apostles. In the south aisle, a figure on horseback may be St. George or St. Gregory, patron saint of Armenia.

The redoubt, composed of a massive tower with three storeys, and erected in 1188, is quite well preserved. The second enclosure wall on the highest point of the hill must be older. What we can see of it belongs to the Byzantine period with restorations by the Arabs and the Armenians.

We then continue towards Kadirli, ancient Flaviopolis, founded under Vespasian, and to KARATEPE an important Hittite site which occupies the summit of a hill overhanging the Ceyhan Valley.

The carvings of Karatepe belong to the last period of the Hittite-Aramaic school and the Phoenician influences which can be seen may establish most of these works as Hittite-Phoenician; this is also borne out by the lively character of the sphinx on the north portal. The influence of Phoenician schools can be seen in the defined tresses of the hair, in the ethnic style with the apron tightly drawn round the body and the epaulettes. We might add that it is a truly frightening creature with flaming eyes encrusted with precious stones.

The hill may have been inhabited since the 12th century, but it was during the 8th century that the kings of Kizzuwatna, or the Hittite realm of Cilicia, erected the fortress of which important vestiges remain. Excavations have brought to light bilingual texts written in Hittite hieroglyphics and in Phoenician. In one of them a king called Azitawadda proclaims himself king of the plain of Cilicia and lord of the Danunas, a people considered as an enemy.

The ruins discovered at the summit of the hill were surrounded by an *enceinte* of about 1,000 metres in perimeter built of huge blocks to a thickness of two to four metres and pierced with two doors. At the top of the hill stood a palace in which several basalt statues have been found. One represented a king with a Phoenician inscription, and there are some orthostats decorated with bas-reliefs, etc. Some of the sculpture has been restored and set up in place again. The raising up of the towers and the curtain wall which links the gates is also in hand and, on one of these, lions and the relief of a ship has been replaced as well as one of the reliefs of the side room to the right.

On the upper door which was decorated with at least four lions and two sphinx with an inscription in Hittite hieroglyphics and in the Semite language, several orthostats have been replaced, in particular a figure seated on a throne, a scene of combat, two scenes of the bringing of tributes, a banqueting scene, animals, divinities, etc.

On another hill called Domuztepe, opposite Karatepe, ruins of a fortress have been discovered which was probably founded before the occupation of Karatepe by the Danunas, by a king of Sam'al. Sparse remains, have been discovered which suggest occupation during the Hellenistic and Roman periods, as well as ruins of the 8th and 9th centuries, including a gate called the Gate of Lions and two buildings with porticoes.

We return to Ceyhan and pass near a medieval fortress, YILAN KALESI, probably built in the reign of Leon II, king of Little Armenia, towards the end of the 12th century near the right bank of the Ceyhan. It is reached through an entrance between two towers. The castle is situated on the north-east section of the rock which dominates the plain in an impressive manner. A ridge of rock strengthens the rest of the cliff and a second *enceinte* protects it to the east.

Further into the plain, there is a second fortress of the same period, Islam Kalesi.

We reach MISIS, a little township on the right bank of the Ceyhan Nahr, ancient *Pyramus*, at the foot of a hill on which used to stand the acropolis of ancient *Mopsuestia*, the *Mamistra* of the Crusaders. The origin of the town goes back to the middle of the 2nd millenium and a rupestral bas-relief near the town testifies to the ascendancy of the Hittites. During the Roman period, Mopsuestia kept a certain autonomy; taken by the Arabs, it was retaken in 965 by Nicephorus Phocas and repopulated by groups of Christians. It was then disputed in several battles between the Armenians and the Byzantines. After having become part of the Armenian kingdom, it remained prosperous in the 13th and 14th centuries and was incorporated into the Ottoman Empire in 1515.

Only sparse vestiges of its stormy past remain to us : some beautiful mosaics at the exit of the town and negligible remains of a Roman amphitheatre.

We then arrive at ADANA, a large flourishing town and one of the most lively in the whole of Turkey. Of ancient foundation, it can be proud of its troubled past, but since practically nothing remains of that past, it is useless to evoke it.

We can, however, visit the Museum which contains some Hittite sculpture, some ceramics of the bronze age, a handsome sarcophagus of the Roman period, etc. We can see, too, some mosques like the *Ramazanoglu Camii* with its beautiful portal of yellow stone built in the 15th century in the Syrian style, or the *Ulu Camii* of the 16th century built of black and white stone and enlarged in 1519 and 1541. Geometric designs decorate the arches of the porticoes and windows. The courtyard is surrounded by a gallery. Behind the mosque, the *Akça Mesçiti* of the beginning of the 15th century, is of interest for its doorway and its mimber.

Finally the *taş Köprü*, built in the 2nd century by the Emperor Hadrian, but repaired several times, in particular under Justinian in the 6th century, has 21 arches of which 14 are still almost intact.

We continue towards TARSUS, the birthplace of St. Paul, which has also become a lively city. It stretches partly over a hill where borings have brought about the discovery of a Hittite site.

A Greek legend tells us that Tarsus had been founded by the

Argians in search of Io, a legend which may go back to the
time of the Peoples of the Sea. But Tarsus was already an
important Hittite city at that time. Annexed to the Assyrian
empire it was taken by Alexander the Great, who nearly died
there after a malignant fever caught when bathing in the
Cydnos. It fell into the hands of Seleucus Nicator I after
Alexander's death and then became a large intellectual metropolis where the greatest masters of the Stoic philosophy taught.
Rejoined to the Roman Empire in 64 B.C., it developed into
a very prosperous port and became covered with monuments
of which, alas, there remain only a few vestiges. Captured and
sacked by the Persians, it lost many inhabitants who were
taken captive to Susiana. When Christianity became the State
religion, Tarsus was the seat of an important bishopric. Occupied by the Arabs in 831, retaken in 965 by Nicephorus
Phocas, it ended by becoming part of the Armenian empire
of Cilicia until 1375. It was in the cathedral at Tarsus that
Leon II was crowned by Conrad von Wittelsbach, legate of
Pope Celestin II in 1169. Tarsus was attached to the Mameluke
Empire in 1359 and, in 1515, to the Osmanli.

We see at Tarsus on the road to Mersin an old Roman
gate caled the Gate of St. Paul, the remains of thermal baths,
of a stoa, of a theatre and, more important, the *Eski Cami*,
which is a former paleo-christian church transformed into a
Gothic church with three aisles separated by arcades in tiercepoint, and then into a mosque with a minaret to the right of
a façade where it is possible to trace the former portal.

The *Ulu Camii* is a mosque of the Abasside period founded
on the site of a temple and preceded by a high portal.

We continue towards MERSIN, another prosperous city,
which has nothing of interest to offer despite its Hittite origin.

A dozen kilometres further on we go past the site of ancient
SOLES founded in 700 B.C. by the Rhodians which is now
occupied by a village called Viransehir.

It is said that Alexander the Great wanted to punish the

inhabitants for not remaining faithful to their Greek origins. They spoke a bastard Greek, from which comes the word "solecism"—to denote errors in syntax—so he imposed a garrison on the town and carried off hostages. It was more likely that he punished them for the city's sympathy with the Persians. To celebrate the Fall of Halicarnassus, Alexander offered up a sacrifice to Asclepius and held Gymnastic displays and musical festivals at Soles. Destroyed by Tigranes the Great, King of Armenia, in 91 B.C. it was rebuilt towards the middle of the 1st century B.C. by Pompey and took the name of *Pompeiopolis* in his honour.

We can see, emerging from the bushes and the fields of maize, a whole row of columns with Corinthian capitals; and there are 23 more which line the main street of the city going from the road to the port to one of the moles which had an eliptical plan. Not only have no excavations been carried out, but building developments are being undertaken close to the portico which originally had 200 columns. This is very much to be regretted. It is obvious that excavations would reveal many other elements of the ancient city which had an acropolis situated to the north.

This whole coast is strewn with ruins. Forty kilometres further on we pass near the site of another ancient town, LAMUS, called Lamas in Byzantine times, situated at the frontier of Cilica Campestris and the Cilicia Aspera. Christians and Moslems used to exchange prisoners on the bridge across the Lamas Cayi in the 9th century, the Christians crying *"Kyrie Eleison"* whilst the Moslems replied, *"Allah Akbar"* (Allah is great).

After another 5 kilometres, the little village of Ayasis to be found on the site of ancient *ELOEUSA* is of Hittite origin since the archives of Bogazköy mention it under the name of *Vilusa*. It was a nest of pirates annihilated by Pompey. The town and the region were given by Augustus in 20 B.C. to King Archelaus I of Cappadocia who built himself a palace there and renamed it Sebaste in honour of Augustus. Annexed by Antiochus IV Commagene in 38, and returned to the Roman Empire in 74, it was represented by a bishop at the Council of Chalcedonia in 454.

To the right of the road, we can see a temple constructed on a terrace of the Roman period. There remains a part of the foundations and of the stylobate, and, on the site of this temple of the Corinthian Order, a little church was built in the 5th century which has traces of a mosaic pavement. We find to the north-west the entrance to an underground chamber.

On the other side of the road near the peninsula are remains of several different antique buildings : *therme*, a theatre, a paleo-christian church etc., which should be in a better state.

Further on we see an aqueduct of the Roman period which used to take water from the springs in the hills of Eloeusa, then we cross a small river near which we can see a little *türbe*.

A road to the right leads to ancient *NEAPOLIS*, also called Kanliderare, founded in the 5th century by Theodosius II who was emperor from 408 to 450 and the author of the Code of Theodosius. After being occupied by the Armenians, it was destroyed and abandoned. One can gauge its importance by the different paleo-christian churches which still subsist, of which some are quite well preserved, with a narthex with three arcades and three aisles ending in an apse with twin windows. The jambs and the lintels of the private houses bear engraved carvings of the sun or a bunch of grapes.

In a chasm in the middle of the town there is a bas-relief cut in the rock which may be Hittite with several bearded figures wearing robes.

A road to the right, which continues as far as Karaman and Konya and which we will describe in the next itinerary, goes through SILIFKE, only a kilometre away, which has a fortress built by the Armenians on a high hill overlooking the shore.

Ancient *Seleucia of Calycadnos* was founded by Seleucus I at the beginning of the 3rd century B.C. It lies 5 kilometres to the south of the present town along the road to Anamur but only amounts to some scattered vestigial remains near a round tower.

It was in the waters of Calycadnis, the present Göksu which we cross, that the emperor Frederick Barbarossa was drowned in 1190.

We then come to the Land Castle of **KORIGOS** built towards the 12th century by the Armenian kings of the Rubenian dynasty, using materials from ancient Byzantine and Roman ruins. The enclosure wall is relatively well-preserved with its square towers dominated by the remains of a keep and the impressive arcade of the main entrance flanked by two consols.

The Castle is built on the edge of the shore and extended into the sea by a Sea Castle on an islet about 100 metres from the shore which used to be connected to the land by a dyke which is now destroyed.

On the other side of the road we see the remains of a cathedral and two churches which go back to the 5th or 6th century, and tombs of an ancient necropolis. This necropolis belonged to ancient *Corycos* which was a pirates' stronghold until it was destroyed by Pompey in 67 B.C.

All along the route we can also see a number of antique remains intermingled with more recent ones.

A road to the right, which crosses the ruins of ancient *Paperon* where we can see the apse of a church, takes us 1·50 kilometres further on to two enormous naturel chasms. The first, reached by means of a steep path, has at the entrance to a cave, the ruins of a little paleo-christian chapel of the 5th century. It has lost its roof and the walls have small windows with slender columns. An inscription in Armenian is engraved on the lintel of the door and the apse, flanked by two sacristies, is covered with a vault bearing scant traces of frescoes.

A little further on, another path leads to the *Necropolis of Kaya* where a tomb of the Roman period may be that of St. Thecla, virgin and martyr, who was born in Iconium (Konya) in the 1st century and was one of the first Christians converted by the preaching of St. Paul.

Near here stood a great basilica dedicated to St. Thecla but only a large section of the wall of the apse remains where the triumphal arch has a span of not less than 13·5 metres. It seems that this important basilica was built by the Emperor Zeno shortly after 476.

Nearby is a well-preserved cistern with two aisles and, a little further on, the remains of another domed church, also dating from the first half of the 5th century.

We then pass near a small fortress which stands on a promontory, Liman Kalesi, then along a pretty beach in a bay. This is a lovely road often running above the sea with splendid prospects.

Beyond the *Castle of Softa Kalesi* which has kept its *enceinte* with towers and, nearby, the remains of *therme* and a Byzantine church, we come to the most splendid fortress of the whole coast, the castle of ANAMUR, also known as the *Mamuri Kalesi*. It was built towards 1230 on a rock which juts out near the coast by the Karamanoğullare, the Emirs of Karaman, on the site of a fortress founded in the middle of the 3rd century.

The entrance, which still has its tierce-point arch, leads into a first courtyard with a redoubt constructed on a rock and, to the right, a second larger courtyard where there is a mosque, a fountain and a bathing pool, etc.

In the left corner on the seaward side stands a keep. The whole fortress can be seen from the top of this tower. The outer walls are very well-preserved with their square or rounded towers with a few loopholes. One of them has a scroll with an inscription. We then find the little village of Anamur and the track which leads to ancient *Anemurium* with its ruins crowning a rocky promontory with walls which protected the town and the acropolis and continue right down to the sea. The remains of a theatre, of an odeon, of two aqueducts and of a necropolis are still visible.

Ten kilometres further on are the ruins of a little fortress which occupies the site of ancient *Platanistous*.

Another 40 kilometres further on, in the outskirts of the village of Kaladran, stands the fortress of Kaladran built by the Byzantines on the site of ancient *Charadrous*.

The road continues to climb above the sea and into a wooded, beautiful mountainous region which it leaves just before reaching the little fishing port of Gazipasa, not far from ancient *Selinous* and 5 kilometres from *Cestrus*, another town of antiquity. We can see a few remains of this latter city such as strips of wall, several buildings and, more particularly, a little temple consecrated to the imperial cult standing between two eminences. On the acropolis are some rupestral niches which used to hold statues.

Another acropolis, 10 kilometres further on to the left, is ancient *Syedra*, now called Demirthas. It is very much ruined. The town occupied a vast area overgrown with bushes out of which emerge the remains of ramparts and a ruined church built of antique materials.

We finally come to the bay of Alanya with, immediately to the left, the International Motel considered to be the best along this coast and, in the background, striped by many lines of fortifications, the rock of ALANYA, a curious cut-off promontary crowned with a citadel which was for many years a lair of pirates.

Ancient *Coracesium* had been transformed into an island by pirates who cut a canal. The fortress, built by Diodorus Tryphon, was captured and destroyed by Pompey during the war against Mithridates. The city was quite unimportant until it was captured in 1220 by the Seljuk sultan, Ala et Tin Kaykobat, who called it Alaiyye (the noble, the exalted) and built himself a winter palace there, then a maritime arsenal which is still visible at the foot of the citadel. It came under the control of the independent Emirs, then under the Karamans, and was sold by them to the Egyptians in 1426. It was

taken by the Ottomans in 1471. The military port remained
very active in the 16th century, the surrounding woods being
exploited intensively for pitch and resin needed by the navy.

The port which we see first is charming, dominated by the
Red Tower *Kizil Kule*, a beautiful edifice built in 1226 in the
reign of the Seljuk Sultan, Ala et Tin Kaykobat, by an architect
from Aleppo, Abou ibn Abir-Rakka el Kettani. This adroit
defensive work which displays the scientific skill of the Syrians
was erected to protect the arsenal and the port after the occupation of the coast by Syria and of Palestine by the Franks.

The red tower is linked to the upper citadel by a long wall
which winds up the precipitous side of the promontory. There
are at least 146 towers and three fortresses in the different projections of the promontory which is now sprinkled with little
red roofed houses.

After going through an old town gate dating from 1226,
near which girls offer pieces of local handmade silk for sale,
we leave, to the right, the acropolis with fortifications built
by the Byzantines and the Seljuks and we enter the upper
citadel by a gateway in a rectangular tower. Opposite, a little
Byzantine church dedicated to St. George still has its dome.
We also see traces of cisterns and shops.

We should notice also, in the northern sector, the *Suleymaniye Camii* reconstructed in the 12th century near the
Akşebe Mesçit of 1230 and of a huge Seljuk edifice with an
interior courtyard, and a former barracks transformed into a
bedestan.

Another mosque, *Andizli*, was constructed in 1277 by the
Emir Bedrüddin.

From the port, boats run excursions to two or three caves
which have no great interest, but another cave, to be found
near the shore on the other side of the promontory, the cave
of Damlatas, has stalactites and stalagmites. It is recommended
for asthmatics and sufferers from chronic bronchitis.

We return to the road to Antalya, leaving to the right the

Sarapsa Hani, a fortified caravanserai constructed in the reign of Kayhosrow between 1236 and 1246. The last bay of this building formed a mosque separated from the rest of the caravanserai by a wall. The entrance, which is to the north and on the side of the road, is well-preserved.

Further on, a road to the left takes us to the ruins of *SIDA* 4 kilometres away. This ancient port, founded after the beginning of the 1st millenium by Aeolian settlers from Cyme was taken by Alexander the Great in 333 B.C. and given a Macedonian garrison because it had forgotten its Greek origin. According to Polybius, at the naval battle of Sida the right wing of the fleet of Antiochus III was formed of vessels supplied by the city but this did not prevent a Rhodian victory. Sida was already a famous slave market and the inhabitants indulged in piracy. Forced to give up piracy after the Pax Romana and to take to commerce they continued to prosper, as can be seen by the many monuments dating from this period.

The prosperity of the town began to diminish after the 2nd century during the first Arab incursions on the shores of Pamphylia; it was the seat of a bishopric in Byzantine times but went into complete decline during the 12th century.

To the left are some ruins of an ancient aqueduct before we reach the landward ramparts which completely cut off entrance to the peninsula and are in an excellent state of preservation with their square, circular or semi-circular projecting towers reaching a height of from 12 to 15 metres. The curtain walls vary between 48·5 metres and 76 metres.

We enter the town through the Great Gate formed of two semi-circles enclosing the actual entrance and preceded by two square towers. They are made of blocks of breccia in rows ·55 metres wide and without mortar. In Imperial Roman times, in the second half of the second century, they were converted into a monumental gateway and the façade was decorated with two rows of niches.

Opposite lie the ruins of an imposing structure which an

inscription terms a *Temple of the Nymphs*. It is a kind of monumental water tower with a façade with three storeys. This is 52 metres long and, preserved to a height of 12 metres, has three semi-circular niches. The sides have only two storeys. A pool in front of this tower can hold 500 cubic metres of water. There is a broad paved terrace in front of the monument surrounded by steps on three sides. The entire frontage is faced with marble.

A street a kilometre long leads to the theatre, whilst another, to the left, leads to the sea. It was lined with porticoes and passed in front of a Byzantine basilica on the plan of an inscribed Greek cross with a narthex opening on the outside by three portals. It occupies the *bema* of a more ancient church with an apse which still partly subsists. To the west, the ruins of an oblong structure may have been the refectory of a monastery of which the church was a sanctuary. To the south of this hall two square structures with four radiating apses intercommunicate.

The basilica was built before the 9th century and must have been one of the earliest known examples of a church on the plan of an inscribed Greek cross with four columns.

If we now follow the road to the theatre we can distinguish in the ground the bases of columns of porticoes and in certain places, vestiges of mosaic pavements which embellished the galleries.

To the right some ancient baths have been converted into a museum which contains some beautiful sarcophagi of the Roman era, statues, fragments of architecture and a great basalt cauldron of the 7th century B.C.

Near the theatre there is a gate in the second small *enceinte*. It masks the wall of the *scena* as it runs down to the south side of the peninsula. To the left, an elegant little monument was set up in Vespasian's time.

In front of the theatre the *agora*, which is square in plan, was lined with porticoes on all four sides. Near the centre, the remains of a rotunda in white marble on a travertine base seems to go back to the Roman period. Corinthian columns supported a coffered roof decorated with the twelve signs of the Zodiac.

The theatre, which is the best preserved building in Sida, is one of the largest of Asia Minor. Built on flat ground it has the peculiarity that its huge *cavea* of 119 metres in diameter is not backed by a hill like the one which we shall soon see at Aspendus, but constitutes, for more than half its height, an independent building like the amphitheatres of the western Roman empire. The tiers of seats, 48 in number, are divided into two sections whilst the radiating stairways are ten in number in the lower part and 24 in the upper part. The auditorium could hold more than 15,000 spectators.

The *cavea* is surrounded by two vaulted superimposed galleries. The lower one formed of 23 arcades, is preserved in its entirety, even though the other one is completely destroyed. The *praecinctio* is surrounded by another gallery which is now open but was probably formerly closed by a wall with doors.

The orchestra, still cluttered up with the materials of the *scena*, is separate. The façade had gates decorated with niches and two rows of columns with Corinthian capitals with heads of the Medusa as well as tragic and comic masks which are all jumbled up on the ground. A frieze, with reliefs which are quite well-preserved in places, decorated the whole length of the stage at a height of 1·50 metres.

After having visited the theatre, we continue along the later ramparts to reach a great rectangular courtyard lined with Ionic colonnades and bounded to the east by a vast vestibule flanked by two smaller rooms. The walls were decorated with niches and covered with a facing of marble for two thirds of their height. The niches were filled with statues of people larger than life, of which about 20 have been preserved. We should notice the bust of a Roman emperor which may perhaps be Gordian III the Pious (238–242) and a statue of a draped woman holding a serpent who could be the goddess

Higieia. Other statues of gods are fine copies of works of
ancient Greece, among them statues of Apollo, Ares, Hermes,
Asklepios, Heracles, Nike and Nemesis.

We then come to the portals of the temple at the southern
extremity of the peninsula, either by returning via the theatre
or by following along the sea ramparts. In either case, we first
come to a semi-circular structure in a courtyard lined with
porticoes on 3 sides. This funerary temple is composed of a
pronaos with two rows of four Corinthian columns, with a
Syrian type frontage and a rectangular cella decorated with
sculptures and plaques and, on the inner and outer sides, with
slabs of marble. This temple, which dates from the end of the
3rd century, or the beginning of the 4th century B.C. stood
next to another tomb of the 3rd century which also had a
courtyard surrounded with a wall and a richly decorated
façade on the seaward side.

On going through the village, we should notice a substructure in the form of a circle preceded by a stairway which
may have served as the base of a little Roman temple. The
foundations of a Byzantine *nymphaeum* used to be nearby.
We are at the end of a great paved way formerly lined with
porticoes which linked this quarter to the theatre.

We then pass in front of the ruins of a Byzantine basilica
with three aisles. When it was destroyed, probably in the 9th
century, a little chapel with one apse and a cruciform dome
was constructed on the east end. The atrium of this basilica used
to cover almost completely the site of two Corinthian temples
planned parallel to each other. Each comprised a *pronaos in
antis* and a *cella* but no opisthodome. Practically nothing
remains except the stylobate which supported the columns and
fragments of sculptures. One of them, dedicated to Athena,
was the most celebrated sanctuary of the town, and from the
3rd century B.C. games were organized here in honour of the
goddess. The smaller one was probably dedicated to Apollo.

Further on, near one of the two ancient harbours, now silted

up, there is an imposing structure in ruins which may have
been a bathing establishment.

Two artificial ports situated on either side of the promon-
tories were enclosed by moles built of great blocks of masonry.
They must have been constantly dredged to avoid being silted
up. A coin of the Imperial Roman era represents a circular
basin lined with porticoes.

We get back to the main road and cross the Copru Cay
over a modern bridge, constructed beside an ancient Seljuk
ass-backed bridge, before coming to the fork for Aspendus
which is 5 kilometres further on.

ASPENDOS, famous for its theatre, one of the best
preserved of the whole of antiquity, was one of the most
important cities of Pamphylia. According to Greek tradition,
it may have been founded by an Argive settler by the name
of Mopsus towards the year 1,000 B.C. It was called *Estwedia*
and stood on a terrace at the place where the Endymion flows
into the coastal plain, a fact which enables it to be, at the
same time, a port and a commercial centre, the river being
navigable as far as Aspendos. The Persian fleet, more than
several hundreds of vessels strong, did not force an entrance
at the time of the great battle which took place in 468
B.C.

Magnificent silver coins decorated with wrestlers, slingers
and horsemen, cast in the city, and antique vases of classical
style, found in the metropolis, bear witness to the importance
of Aspendos at that time. In 333 B.C., Aspendos surrendered
to Alexander the Great on condition that no garrison should
be stationed there. The Macedonian conqueror accepted these
terms but forced them to pay him the tribute which they had
been paying the Persians. As the city did not honour its com-
mitment, he occupied the lower town and imposed harsher
terms. In the year 190, Aspendos surrendered to Rome but
then became allied to Pergamum and did not become Roman
again until the death of Attalus III. Verres pillaged the artistic

29. SIDA : THEATRE

30. ASPENDOS : THEATRE

31 : PERGA : THEATRE

32. ANTALYA : GATE OF HADRIAN

treasures of the city which rebelled against his authority, an action which Cicero deplored.

According to an inscription on one of the main gates, the theatre was erected by the architect Zeno, a native of Aspendos, in the reign of the Emperors Antoninus and Lucius Verus in the 2nd century A.D.

This great work is constructed of a bad conglomerate taken from the neighbouring hills, the tiers of seats, the surroundings of the gates and windows and the pavements are in limestone, whilst the inner façade of the stage was faced with marble slabs which have disappeared. As well as the two main entrances, two other gates communicate with the arcropolis and are cut beneath the gallery which surrounds the upper part of the *cavea*. The tiers are made in a semi-circular enclosure wall of 95·48 metres. They are 19 in number with 21 steps in the upper maenianum and of 20 with 10 stairways in the lower maenianum. The gallery, which surmounts the tiers and rests on some pilasters, is intact, as well as the *vomitorium* and the promenade at the height of the middle *praecinctio*.

The stage building has lost the major part of its interior ornamentation which comprised two rows of columns, Ionic below and Corinthian above, broken in the centre with a pediment flanked by three balconies supporting an entablature. On the outside the façade is absolutely intact with the exception of the cornice which has disappeared.

The rest of the ruins of Aspendos are of no great importance. Besides a little rupestral tomb with a vestibule leading on to a funerary chamber with a niche, we can see the acropolis which extends over two steep hills, and by means of which we reach the three gates. At the summit, the ruins of the agora are insignificant. They were lined to the west by shops preceded by a portico and to the east by a basilica. We can see to the north the remains of a *nymphaeum* where the walls still stand up to a height of 15 metres and are 35 metres long. The façade on the *agora* side is decorated with two rows superimposed by five niches, the one in the centre on the lower storey having a gate.

To the east a vast structure spans a ravine by three semi-circular arches.

Finally to the north of the city a whole system of aqueducts used to bring water from the hills. A little valley is crossed by an aqueduct with a single row of arcades between two hydraulic towers of about 30 metres, at the top of which the water arrived by crossed arches to flow down again on the other side. The water, under strong pressure, could rise up to pour into a little tank where air restraining the flow of water along the pipes could escape. The water then flowed down again in limestone conduits which carried it to the acropolis.

For those who are not dismayed at the prospect of riding and walking long distances, it is possible by going to Beskonak 46 kilometres away to reach the site of another great city of Pamphylia, *SELGE*, with its imposing ruins near the village of Zerk. We follow the old mule track cut in the rock in a region of deep and precipitous ravines which Strabo says "prevented the city from being subject to any other country for all time". We see there in a magnificent setting, the remains of walls of a theatre, of an *agora*, of a stadium, of several temples and churches. The necropolis has numerous sarcophagi.

We go back to the main road and we leave, to the right, a track for the acropolis of *SILLIUM*, today called Yanköy, 15 kilometres away. This ancient town, probably founded by Greek settlers at the same time as the neighbouring cities of Perga and Aspendus was besieged in 33 B.C. by Alexander the Great.

The track runs at a short distance along the Ak Çay and it is just negotiable by car. Then after about 15 kilometres, we must make our way across fields for about an hour towards the ancient town found to the right at the top of a large hillock. The remains are almost all from early times and are gathered

round the acropolis which occupies a height in the centre of
the plateau. We reach this by means of two ramps, partly cut
in the rock. The northern one leads to a monumental gate
formed of a square of six metres with two entrances three
metres wide. The southern ramp goes up with a gentle slope
between two walls and meets the first one on the terrace before
reaching the *agora*.

We can make out, on the western side of the hill in particular, foundations of ancient dwelling places comprising two
or three rooms with doors and steps cut in the stone. Several
cisterns have been found with quadrangular or semi-circular
entrances closed by a screen with another smaller entrance.
Conduits cut in the rock flow into the reservoirs.

The theatre occupies the western slope. The stage has disappeared but 15 tiers of seats are still visible. An *odeon* adjoins
the theatre.

As well as the walls, we should also look at the ruins of the
Hellenistic era to the north-west among which is a temple.

After having crossed the Ak Çay, we reach Aksu and from
here a road to the right takes us to another ancient village,
PERGA, two kilometres away. It was founded at the beginning
of the 1st millennium in the period of emigration of the
Achaeans in Pamphylia. Originally laid out on a hill, it
stretched at the foot of the acropolis in Persian times, and the
lower town was the more important after the conquest of
Alexander the Great. The city did not resist him and during the
Hellenistic era it became an important town surrounded with
powerful ramparts by the Seleucid kings. Its sanctuary
dedicated to Artemis was famous. In 188 B.C. it was besieged
and taken by the Romans. St. Paul and St. Barnabas sojourned
there. It continued to prosper under Roman domination and
became covered with magnificent monuments of which the
theatre was one. It was still inhabited in Byzantine times.

We should begin our visit to the theatre which backs against
a hill to the left of the road. The *cavea* could hold 15,000

N*

spectators. It was divided by a medial *praecinctoria* into
triangular sections by radiating steps. As at Aspendos, a partly
ruined gallery surrounded the upper part and four vaulted
galleries opened out onto the *praecinctoria*. With its 49 tiers
of seats, the *cavea* could hold 12,000 spectators. The stage, 56
metres long and 4·40 metres wide, is still partly ruined and
the debris half hides the wall of the stage. To the right the
separate section has magnificent bas-reliefs surmounted by
columns of which we can see the bases and, between, there
were gates with delicactely carved frames.

On the ground floor, a large hall is cluttered up with masonry
and the structure of the stage is decorated outside with five
great niches.

On the other side of the road, the well-preserved stadium is
234 metres long and the track is 34 metres wide. The tiers of
seats mount up in a horseshoe of 12 rows resting on powerful
vaulted foundations. Whereas the southern extremity was
rectilineal, the stadium terminates to the north in a semi-circle.
The monumental entrance to the south has disappeared.

On the other side of the oval courtyard stands a Triumphal
Arch of two storeys on a platform reached by four steps. It was
erected during the reign of Hadrian, between A.D. 117 and 121
by Plancia Magna, daughter of Marcus Plancius Varus,
governor of Bithynia. It was composed of four massive pillars
linked by arches, and niches with statues were hollowed out
of the side pillars, whilst the two others were decorated with
little columns resting upon a high pedestal.

The Triumphal Arch opens onto a paved way lined with
porticoes which goes up to the entrance of the Acropolis. To
the right of the avenue stands a marble column decorated with
a relief depicting Artemis of Perga holding bows and arrows
in her left hand and a torch in the other. On another column
there is a rather worn relief of Apollo and a third depicts a man
in a toga pouring a libation over an altar. These three columns
were re-used in the construction of a Byzantine church.

Beyond, on the first slopes of the acropolis, the ruins of a building comprising a vast courtyard lined with porticoes may have been a gymnasium constructed by Julius Cornutus and his wife in honour of the Emperor Claudius. The ruins of a Byzantine edifice overlap the northern section of the structure.

A single gateway led to the acropolis where, amongst sparse ruins, stand the remains of a Byzantine church with three aisles constructed of more ancient materials.

To the north-west of the city, recent excavations have brought to light some beautiful sarcophagi of Imperial Roman times.

We soon reach ANTALYA, the most important city of the whole coast. Its mild climate makes it a winter and touristic resort with a big future. It is altogether delightful, set in a fertile plain, watered by numerous streams which flow down from the slopes of the Taurus mountain. Orchards and palm groves surround its picturesque little fishing port with old houses dominated by a fluted minaret. Comfortable hotels and motels have been built in the nearby creeks.

Antalya was founded in the 2nd century B.C. by Attalus II, king of Pergamum, to whom the Romans gave the sovereignty of Pamphylia after the battle of Magnesia ad Sipylum. In A.D. 195, it was surrounded with strong walls, whilst the province was declared the seat of a senate. These ramparts were reinforced by the emperors, Leo VI and Constantine Porphyrogenetes, and, during the crusades, *Attaleia* which the crusaders called *Satalia*, became an important place from which the knights re-embarked for Palestine. Joined up again in 1207 to the estates of the Sultan of Roum, it then came under the control of the sultans of Karaman before being incorporated into the Ottoman Empire at the end of the 14th century.

We shall begin our visit with the archaeological museum housed in a former church transformed into a mosque and embellished with its celebrated fluted minaret of brick with the upper part decorated with little cubes of blue faience. The

Yivli Minare was erected at the beginning of the 13th century by the Seljuk Sultan, Ala et Tin Kaykobat.

We first of all see in the garden a little *türbe* of the Seljuk period and, to the right, the old library. In the museum we should notice more particularly a beautiful sarcophagus from Perga with bas-reliefs depicting the labours of Hercules, another decorated with a recumbent figure of the Sidamarran type also from Perga, statuettes, a Byzantine reliquary from Demre, two paleo-christian mosaics, etc.

The most remarkable structure of Antalya is the Gate of Hadrian, the old white marble gate of the city, attributed to this emperor. Its barrel vaults are decorated with panels with rosettes and flowers. The entablature is sumptuously embellished with garlands, acanthus, ovoids and lions' heads.

The tower to the left, of the Roman era and 14 metres high, bears an inscription on the outside stating that this bastion was constructed at the expense of Julia Sancta.

The right hand tower was restored at the beginning of the 10th century in the reign of Constantine Porphyrogenetes.

As well as several vestiges of the *enceinte*, we can see, on the edge of the cliff overlooking the port, a round tower of the Roman period constructed in well-dressed masonry on a square base with a room on the lower floor.

Finally we should drive to the truncated minaret, *Kesik Minare*, a former church consecrated in the 5th century to the Panaghia, which was restored several times before being adapted for Moslem worship in the 13th century.

Probably reconstructed during the 7th century, it was preceded by a narthex and the nave terminated in a semi-circular apse. Antique materials, dating from the 2nd century were re-used in its construction as can be seen in the lintel of a little door.

The *Karatay Camii*, built in the middle of the 13th century by a Seljuk vizier called Karatay, has an interesting entrance and a *mihrab* decorated with stalactites.

GLOSSARY

ABACUS : Flat slab on top of a capital.

ABUTMENT : Solid masonry placed to resist the lateral pressure of a vault.

ACANTHUS : Plant with thick fleshy and scalloped leaves copied as part of decoration of a Corinthian capital and in some types of leaf-carving.

ACROTERION : Pedestal for a statue at the angle of the pediment.

ADYTON : Inner sanctuary.

AEDICULE : Small structure sheltering altar or image of household god; small pedimented structure over a niche.

Aghiasma: Holy spring for purification.

AGORA : Market Place.

ALEIPTERION : Chamber for athletes' anointing at gymnasia.

ANTA : A pilaster terminating the side wall of a Greek temple with the base and capital differing from those of adjacent columns.

AMBULATORY : Open or covered arcade or cloister; an aisle around a choir.

ANTIPHONARY : Book of chants or anthems.

APSE : Eastern end of church containing Bishop's Throne.

APSIDIOLE : Secondary apse.

ARCADE : Range of arches supported on piers or columns, free-standing. BLIND ARCADE : Arcade set against a wall.

ARCATURE : Blind arcade.

ARCHITRAVE : Lowest division of entablature rising on capitals of supporting column. Collective name for various parts surrounding a door or window.

ARCHIVOLT : Moulding curving round the under surface of an arch.

ARCOSOLIUM : Ancient form of tomb, hollowed out of rock beneath an arch.

ARKOSE : Rock composed of quartz and felspar.

ARMARIUM : Cupboard or chest.

ASHLAR : Square, hewn stone.

ASTRAGAL : Small moulding round top or bottom of column.

ATRIUM : Open central Court in Greek and Roman buildings; forecourt in early Christian churches.

BALDACHIN : Canopy, supported on pillars or fastened to wall, over throne, pulpit, altar, etc.

BARBICAN : Outwork defending the entrance to a castle.

BAROQUE : Style with sinuous lines, scrolls and exuberant carved ornaments, named after the painter Federigo Barocci, from Urbino (1528–1612). Born in Rome as a reaction against severe classical Renaissance, it spread throughout Europe.

BARTIZAN : Turret projecting from mediaeval tower.

BASILICA : In mediaeval architecture an aisled church with a clerestory.

BAS-RELIEF : Figures not standing far out from ground on which they are formed.

BATTEN : Long, thin piece of squared timber used for flooring or hanging roof tiles.

BAYS : Internal compartments of a building; each divided from the other not by solid walls but by divisions only marked in the side walls. Also external divisions of a building by fenestration.

Bedestan: Covered Bazaar.

BELVEDERE : Raised turret from which to view scenery.

BEMA : Speaker's Tribune, or Platform.

BILLET MOULDING : Ornamental moulding consisting of small cylindrical blocks arranged in a sunken moulding.

BOULEUTERION : Council chamber.

BUCRANE : Sculptured ornament representing ox skull.

BUTTRESS : Projecting support built on to outside of wall.

CABOCHONS : Precious stones polished but not cut into facets.

CADUCEUS : Mercury's wand.

Caldarium: Hot room in Roman baths.

CALOTTE : Skull cap, applied to a detail of this shape.

Camii: Mosque.

CAMPANILE : Isolated bell-tower.

CAPITAL : Moulded or carved top of column.

CARYATID : Whole figure supporting an entablature or other similar member.

CASEMATE : Vaulted chamber in thickness of fortress-wall, with embrasures for defence.

CAVEA : Auditorium of open-air theatre.

CELLA : Main body of a classical temple, excluding the portico.

CENSER : A vessel in which incense is burned.

CENSE : The act of burning incense.

CHALICE : Cup used in Communion service or at Mass.

CHAMFER : Surface produced by bevelling square edge or corner equally on both sides—moulding.

CHAMPLEVÉ ENAMEL : Work in which the metal ground is hollowed out and spaces filled with enamel.

CHAPTER HOUSE : Meeting place of members of religious order.

CHASUBLE : The outer vestment of the celebrant at Mass.

CHEVET : Apsidal east end of church.

CHRESMOGRAPHEION : Chamber for writing down oracles.

CHRISMA : A monogram of Christ formed by the letters χ and ρ.

CIBORIUM : Vessel similar to chalice in which the Host is deposited. Canopy over high altar.

CINQUEFOIL : Arch or circular opening divided into five lobes or leaves by projecting carving.

CIPPUS : Roman term for monumental pillar.

CISTERCIAN : Order founded in 1098 in Burgundy, at Cîteaux (Latin *Cistercium*) near Dijon, and which received a great impulse under St. Bernard, founder of the Abbey of Clairvaux. The monasteries of this Order express by their architecture the severity of the rule (more austere form of Benedictine rule).

CLEPSYDRA : Vessel through which water trickled for the purpose of measuring time.

CLERESTORY : Upper storey with rows of windows.

COFFER : Deep panel in ceiling, vault or dome.

CONSOLE : Ornamental bracket used to support cornices on which to place busts, vases or figures.

COPE : Ecclesiastical vestment worn over surplice.

CORBEL : Block of stone projecting from a wall, supporting some horizontal feature.

CORNICE : Uppermost member of entablature, surmounting the frieze.

COUNTERSCARP : Outer wall or slope of ditch, supporting covered way.

CRENEL : Open space of a battlement.

CROCKET : Carved ornament on angles of spires and on canopies.

CROSSING : That part of a cruciform church where the transepts cross the nave.

CUFIC : Pertaining to Cufa, a town on the Euphrates, south of Babylon; applied especially to an Arabic alphabet earlier employed there.

CULVERIN : Small firearm; large cannon, very long in proportion to its bore, used especially in 16th and 17th centuries.

CUPOLA : Spherical vault or concave ceiling.

CYCLOPEAN : Style of masonry with walls of large, irregular stones, unhewn and uncemented, which in ancient Greece were fabled to be the work of Cylops, or one-eyed giants.

DIACONICUM : Vestry.

DIAZOMA : Cornice or frieze.

DRIP-STONE : Projecting moulding to throw off rain.

DRUM OR TAMBOUR : Upright part of a cupola.

Enceinte: An enclosing wall of fortifications.

ENGAGED : Built into. ENGAGED COLUMN : Column built into wall.

ENTABLATURE : Arrangements of horizontal members above supporting columns.

ENTASIS : Convex tapering of a column.

EPHEBES : Devotees.

EXEDRA : Apsidal end of a room.

FAÇADE : Face or front of building.

FAÏENCE : Decorated glazed earthenware.

FINIAL : Ornamental feature placed on top of pinnacle or at base and apex of gable.

FRIGIDARIUM : Cold room in Roman bath.

FLAMBOYANT : Late form of the Gothic style, characteristic for its "florid" enrichments of carved ornament, and for the "flaming" arrangements of the window stonefilling.

FLUTING : Vertical channelling in the shaft of a column.

FOIL : Lobe formed by the cusping of a circle or an arch. Trefoil, quatrefoil, cinquefoil, multifoil, express number of leaf shapes to be seen.

FOLIATED : Carved with leaf shapes.

FRESCO : Painting on plastered wall before plaster has dried.

FRIEZE : Middle division of a classical entablature.

GALLERY : In church architecture, upper storey above an aisle, opened in arches to the nave.

GALLO-ROMAN : Belonging to the epoch when Gaul was a part of the Roman Empire (1st–4th century).

GLACIS : Bank slopping down from fort, on which attackers are without cover from gunfire.

GOTHIC : Style which appeared in France in the 12th century, and prevailed in Europe from the 13th to the 15th centuries. Its chief elements are the vault with diagonal ribs with pointed arches and flying buttresses.

GROIN : Sharp edge at the meeting of two cells of a cross-vault.

Hammam: Turkish bath.

Han: Inn.

HELICOIDAL : Resembling a snail shell; spiral ornament.

HIERATISM : Priestly tradition that made Byzantine art too rigid.

HIGH GOTHIC : *see* Flamboyant.

HISTORIATED : Adorned with figures.

Hôtel: Large house or mansion, in addition to meaning as in English hotel.

HYPOGEUM, HYPOSTYLE : Underground room or vault.

Imaret: Hospice for the poor.

IMBRICATED : Overlapping.

IMPLUVIUM : Square basin in the middle of an atrium to receive rainwater.

IMPOST : Brackets in walls, usually formed of mouldings, on which the ends of an arch rest.

In commendum: Ecclesiastical benefice temporarily held in care of clerk.

INTRADOS : Inner curve or underside of an arch.

INTAGLIO : Engraved design; incised carving in hard material.

JAMB : Straight side of an archway, doorway, or window.

JUBE : Screen between nave and chancel (rood-screen).

Kaynarca Hamman: Hot baths.

Küklürtili Hamman: Sulphur baths.

Kulliye: Complex of buildings.

LANCET : Tall, narrow window wth acutely pointed head.

LANTERN : In architecture, a small circular or polygonal turret with windows all round crowning a roof or dome.

LIERNE : Short rib connecting two main ribs.

LINTEL : Horizontal beam or stone bridging an opening.

LOMBARD : Early form of the Romanesque style (9th and 10th centuries) born in Lombardy, Italy.

LOZENGE : Diamond shape.

MACHICOLATION : Projecting gallery or parapet with series of openings for pouring molten substances on attackers below.

MARQUETRY : Inlaid work arranged to form decorative patterns.

Medrese: Moslem theological school.

MERLON: Part of wall of battlement lying between two openings.

METOPE : The square space between two triglyphs in a frieze of a Doric order.

Mezzo-rilievo: Degree of relief in figures halfway between high and low.

Mimber: Pulpit.

MINIATURE : Painting on a very small scale.

Mirhab: Niche in any part of a mosque facing Mecca.

MISERERE : Projection on underside of tilt-up seat in choirstall.

MISERICORD : Room set apart in monastery where monks might take special food as an indulgence : the indulgence or relaxation of monastic rule itself.

MODILLION : Projecting bracket under a cornice in Corinthian and other orders.

MOORISH : Islamic style peculiar to the Moors of Spain (8th–14th century).

Muezzin: The summoner to prayer.

MULLION : Vertical bar of wood or stone dividing window into two or more "lights".

NAISKOS : Shrine.

NAOS : Sanctuary or principal chamber of a Greek temple containing the statue of the god.

NARTHEX : In early Christian architecture, a vestibule forming an entrance to a basilica, originally for women penitents and catechumens.

NAUMACHIA : Sea-fight.

NAVE : Body of church.

NEWEL : Central post in circular or winding staircase; also, principal post when flight of stairs meets a landing.

NIMBUS : Bright cloud or halo investing deity or saint.

Nymphaeum: Roman temple of the nymphs.

OCULUS : Circular or "bull's-eye" window.

ODEON : Building for shows.

OGIVE : Pointed arch or window, with double curve.

OMPHALLOA : Conical stone used by oracles.

OPISTHODOME : Enclosed section at rear of a Greek temple sometimes used as a treasury.

Oppidum: Latin for town.

ORDER : In classic architecture, column with base, shaft, capital, and entablature according to one of the following styles : Greek Doric, Roman Doric, Tuscan Doric, Ionic, Corinthian, Composite. Alternatively an Order of monks.

OVEN-SHAPED : This description is applied to the structures which have the dome shape of the old French bread ovens, e.g. mainly in the case of apses at the eastern end of the church.

PALESTRA : Gymnasium.

PARADOS : Elevation of earth behind fortified place to secure it from rear attack.

PARACCLESION : Chamber for prayer.

PARVIS : Enclosed area in front of church or cathedral.

PATERA : Small flat circular or oval ornament in classical architecture.

PATINA : Encrustation of age to works of art.

PATIO : Courtyard.

PEDIMENT : Low-pitched gable used in classical, Renaissance, and neo-classical architecture above a portico.

PENDENTIVE : Spherical triangle formed between each pair of supporting arches in dome resting on square base.

PERISTYLE : Row of columns round building or courtyard.

PILASTER : Flat column against face of wall.

PINNACLE : Ornamental form crowning a spire, tower, buttress.

PISCINA : Basin for washing the Communion or Mass vessels.

PODIUM : Continuous base of plinth supporting columns.

POLYPTYCH : Picture or carving with many panels.

POROS : Chalky stone.

PORTAL : Gate or doorway.

PREDELLA : In an altar-piece the horizontal strip below the main representation, often used for a number of subsidiary representations in a row.

PRESBYTERY : Part of church reserved for clergy, also dwelling house for clergy.

PRITANAEUM : Public hall.

PRONAOS : Vestibule of a Greek or Roman temple, enclosed by side walls and a range of columns in front.

PROPYLAEA : Entrance gateway to an enclosure.

PROSCENIUM : In a Greek or Roman theatre, the stage on which the action took place.

PROTHESIS : Credence table for Eucharist.

PSALTER : Book of Psalms.

Putto (plural *putti*) : Small naked boy.

Pyxis : Sacred box containing Host after consecration.

Rampart : Defensive bank of earth, with or without stone parapet.

Reliquaries : Chests or caskets containing relics.

Rivak: Arcade surrounding central courtyard of mosque.

Rococo : Late Baroque style with a profusion of rock-like forms, scrolls, crimped shells (from French "rocaille"—"rock work").

Romanesque : Architectural style prevalent in Western Europe towards the end of 12th century, characterised by use of massive stone vaulting and the round-headed arch. Usually known in reference to English buildings as Norman.

Rood-screen : Open screen across chancel entrance in church.

Rose-window : Gothic circular window filled with tracery resembling a rose.

Rotunda : Circular building, usually with domed roof.

Rupestral : Rock.

Sacristy : Part of church where sacred vessels and vestments are kept.

Sarcophagus : Stone receptacle for corpse.

Sardirvan: Ablutions fountain.

Seraglio: Harem.

Serpentine : Decorative stone.

Soffit : Underside of lintels, arch or cornice.

Springer : Bottom stone of arch.

Squinch : Small stone arch across an interior angle of square tower to support octagonal spire.

Stele : Upright monument.

Stereotomy : Art or science of cutting stones into regular forms.

Stoa : Detached colonnade.

Stringcourse : Projecting horizontal moulding or projecting course of stone or brick running across face of building.

Stucco : Plaster work.

Stylobate : Substructure on which a colonnade stands.

Sudatorium : Room for hot-air baths to produce sweating.

Synthronon : Enthronement.

TELAMONES : Carved male figures serving as pillars.

TEMENOS : Sacred precinct.

TEPIDARIUM : Room for warm bath.

TESSERA : Small cube of glass, stone or marble used in mosaic.

TIERCERON : Secondary rib, issuing from main springer or central boss and leading to a ridge rib.

TORUS : Moulding in base of columns with semi-circular profile.

TRACHYTE : Rough-surfaced.

TRANSEPT : Transverse portion of a cross-shaped church.

TRANSOM : Horizontal bar across the openings of a window.

TRIBUNAL : Confessional.

TRIBUNE : Gallery of church.

TRIFORIUM : Arcaded wall passage or blank arcading facing the nave at the height of the roof of the side-aisles and below the clerestory windows.

TRIGLYPHS : Blocks with vertical grooves separating the metopes in a doric frieze.

TRIPTYCH : Picture or carving on three panels.

TUFA : Rock of cellular texture of volcanic origin.

Türbe: Mausoleum.

TYMPANUM : Triangular space between sloping and horizontal cornices above lintel of doorway.

VOLUTE : Spiral scroll.

WAGON-ROOF : Roof in which by closely set rafters with arched braces the appearance of the inside of a canvas tilt over a wagon is achieved.

Zavije: Corner; angle. Holy place for a specific religious sect.

INDEX OF TOWNS AND PLACES VISITED